Two Worlds Apart

BY MARGARET NORMAN

Pen Press

First published in Great Britain by Pen Press

All paper used in the printing of this book has been made from wood grown in managed, sustainable forests.

ISBN13: 978-1-907172-00-7

Printed and bound in the UK
Pen Press is an imprint of Indepenpress Publishing Limited
25 Eastern Place
Brighton
BN2 1GJ

A catalogue record of this book is available from the British Library

Cover design by Jacqueline Abromeit

Chapter 1

Four score years and seven. Have I really lived that long? If, as they say, a lifetime is measured in years, each year holds the minutes of that lifetime where memories are born and stored to be recalled in a second by a word or thought — the mundane, the tragic, the love, the laughter, lean times, good times, peacetime and wartime with its aftermath. It's all there — a patchwork quilt of memories to warm my heart as I drift through them musing, you might care to join me.

I was born in 1920. My first memory is from my bedroom window, overlooking a garden, a plum tree and a swing. The garden belongs to my father and mother. I have my own small but comforting bedroom with a ceiling that slants down to the window. I can lie in bed and watch the clouds and the stars on a clear night. From my window I can look down on an old plum tree — in springtime a mass of blossom, summertime laden with deep purple fruits, and in the autumn the fall of its dry crunchy leaves, which Dad and I rake up for a bonfire in November, but best of all my swing, which hangs from its sturdy branches.

My best friend is Barbara who lives along the lane by my house, we play together every day, and have a little sweetshop with small glass jars filled with dolly mixtures, cashew sweets and small liquorice allsorts. We take it in turn to be shopkeeper. Fortunately, Mum has a secret store of refills tucked away. The amber gum from the plum tree bark we roll into circles to make pretend money. Barbara's two older brothers play football in the lane quite noisily, and they let us join in sometimes. We think it is 'grown up' to learn some of their favourite words.

Gran and Grandad Bartlett, my Dad's parents, come to tea occasionally. Gran is a small quiet lady, very musical, and a very good cook. Grandad is quite a tall man, always happy, with a kind word and a smile. Dad is very like him I think. This afternoon they brought me a big teddy with a kindly face — not all teddies are alike you know! After teatime, when everyone is nicely full up, I venture to join the conversation, including my new vocabulary. The conversation ceases immediately, to my surprise, and all eyes swivel to me. Silence hangs in the air for what seems an endless moment. The consternation of my parents is very apparent, then come the tight-lipped smiles after I have been admonished and things return to normal. I can't understand what all the fuss is about, it must be something dreadful. Grandad gives me a kiss and a smile when they leave and I slip quietly into the garden to dangle my legs on my dear old swing. In despair, I wonder if they have taken the teddy bear back with them. Barbara comes along to console me, and gives the swing a little push, and then for fun she winds me round and round till the swing goes no further, then she lets go and I spin round and round like a spinning top, and when it stops I feel very sick. I think it must be my punishment but I am philosophical and I don't tell anyone. I think it best to keep quiet at the moment and creep back into the house. Yes, my new teddy is still there; he becomes a good friend to me.

Life is mainly uneventful but I am quite happy. The village where we live is composed of small cottages on either side of a steep hill, Frenchay Hill which leads down to the Flock Mills by the side of the River Frome. The road follows the river for a short stretch to a stone bridge, which crosses the river and leads on to Downend.

The village road continues on up a steep hill — Pierces Hill — and then on to Frenchay Common. There had been much stone quarrying in the past, which accounts for the deep drop in the landscape in places. Frenchay is a conservation area and quite lovely. Bordering the Common are many large houses, which in the past were occupied by the Quaker Community and prosperous business families seeking respite from the city of Bristol, the Quakers have their own meeting house and burial ground there. The Meeting House at Frenchay is well known and visited by many Quakers from around the country. I remember going to a meeting with my Gran where I was allowed to take my small piece of knitting to keep me occupied, as talking was not allowed, in fact, there were periods of intense silence for contemplation. We sat on long, wooden seats, which I believe are still in the meeting house to this day. There was also hymn singing in which Gran joined lustily.

The large houses provides work for many of the villagers and the old coach road from Bristol follows the Common down to Becks Pool and the outskirts of Hambrook, connecting all the villages on the way to Winterbourne and Iron Acton. It is a lifeline in the 1900s when the horse and carriage is the mode of transport for the wealthy inhabitants. In these times, the villagers were expected to stop and curtsey or doff their caps as the carriages pass by; my mother is strictly admonished when she failed to curtsey, a fact that was relayed back to Mrs Mann, her mother, and Gran was not amused!

There is only the occasional, slow moving automobile or carriage and pair, so the comparatively smooth surface of the coach road allowed us to play in safety with our brightly chalk-painted spinning tops, hoops and marbles there. Granny Mann lives quite near us, and is very much a part of our lives. She is plump, kind, and good hearted, you would never think of disobeying her. She is a good cook — her sponges are as light as air, and her pea soup brought up to us in a large white china jug, is mouthwatering. Aunt Edie, her eldest daughter, lives with her and Granfer Mann, as she was profoundly deaf. Granfer Mann is gruff but kind and is the gardener for the Frys, who live in a large house at the end of the Common.

To get to Gran's, there is a stone stile at the bottom of our garden, which you sit on and swing one leg over and then the other, then with two feet together jump down to the earth path below, which runs beside a neighbour's house into Gran's house and garden. No one minds this, as all the houses and land belong to the Tucketts. Gran's garden has a well-kept front lawn, where at weekends and bank holidays she serves teas and her homemade cakes and sponges. Mum and I help her with the serving and washing-up.

A popular walk from the surrounding areas on the outskirts of Bristol was through Vassells Park, Oldbury Court, across the river by the stone bridge, turn right up Frenchay Hill to Gran's for a nice cup of tea, then up to the Common and back to the stone bridge via Pierces Hill. *(See map in the back of the book.)*

The Common is lovely, and will always be there as it is common land. The villagers were allowed to keep their animals there, and did so in earlier days. There are two tethered goats, two horses and hens at the moment, the hens are called in at dusk and return to houses through a hole in their garden wall.

Cricket is played there in the summer on Saturday afternoons. WG Fields, captain of Frenchay Cricket Club in 1870 plays there quite often, as he lived only a few miles away at Downend. There is a large tea tent on the Green to serve teas for the players, where my mother often helps out. Wooden seats are set around the playing field for supporters and visitors to watch the play. There was a large wooden scoring board on which metal number plates hang, and are changed as the runs are scored or the wickets go down. My father would take his deckchair and our dog, Bonzo, to watch the game. The Walls' 'Stop Me and Buy One' man with his three-wheeled bicycle and small wagon of ice cream would come every Saturday afternoon for this captive audience. If I was around, Dad would give me a penny for a Walls' 'Snofruit'.

I have a 'Fairy' cycle for my fifth birthday and learnt to ride on two wheels on the narrow path that led from the church. The church stood solemnly surveying the Common, and the modernity of the coach road. I think the path was to facilitate the ladies and gentlemen from the big houses on the way to church. On this path, my father would run behind my bicycle, holding the saddle while I peddled. This is fine and gives me confidence, one day I realise my father has let go and I am cycling on my own. I was excited and turn my head to say 'Look Dad', but of course, I wobble and run off the path onto the grass and the two tethered goats. We are all none the worse for this episode. I will never in all my years lose my love of cycling.

There were several shops in the village, the Post Office is part of Barbara's house, it also sells sweets in jars, and most of the village gossip and news can be obtained here. Further down the hill is an ironmongers, which sells paraffin, candles and nails. There isn't any electricity in most of the houses and paraffin is essential for the oil lamps, our light comes from a brass based lamp with a fine glass funnel which is placed over the lighted wick, with an ornate white glass top to cover it.

At bath time, a long cylindrical galvanized bath is put in front of the kitchen range and partly filled with hot water from large saucepans heating on the range. I was told never to sit on the edge of the bath, but one day, when trying to dry myself, I forget, and I did. Catastrophe! All the water poured out over the kitchen floor — I am sent to bed and cried and cried. Dad, a bit later, puts his head round the bedroom door and says 'Never mind,' but I am inconsolable, and could only say that nobody loves me. The angst of children is underestimated, but it's a learning process — tomorrow is another day and we are all a little wiser — life moves on.

Milk is delivered daily and comes from a local farm at Hambrook. Mr Flux comes by in pony and trap, with the milk in churns, which he ladles into your waiting jug, the butcher calls twice a week. Mrs Baber runs the grocery shop, butter is sold in pats, from a large block, bacon and ham are sliced to size and choice, dried fruits and sugar are weighed up in strong paper bags. The bread is baked by the sons of the Baber family, in ovens below the shop — very nice too. Hot cross buns are specially baked on Good Friday morning. My dad gets up early in the morning to bring them back, still warm, to be buttered and eaten with pleasure. There is a cobbler at the bottom of the hill, small and wizened — he used to frighten me, as I timidly tapped on his door to collect some repaired shoes, a deep voice would say 'Wadya want', but he was probably quite nice really.

My sister Esme is born in December 1925. There seemed so much to think about, so I keep very quiet and melt into the background. The new baby takes over the house, and seems to cry a lot, Mum goes about her work with the baby tucked under her arm, but the new baby became more interesting when her little fingers try to hold mine. Ah well, there is always Barbara to play with and my swing, and I hear Christmas mentioned today! I wonder if there is plum jam for tea? It's my favourite!

Chapter 2

In 1925 Cecil Fry, Granfer's employer, had a modern bungalow built for Gran, Granfer and Aunt Edie on the edge of their estate and fronting on to the far end of the Common, by Becks Pool. The bungalow was ideal for them and had a bathroom with hot and cold running water, an Aga-type kitchen range, which didn't need black leading, two bedrooms, a comfortable sized sitting room, and a large practical kitchen with plenty of room for meals around a large, well-scrubbed wooden table. The view from the wide window was to the fields beyond. We loved those fields at all times of the year, the nodding moon daisies when the grass was high in May, and haymaking time in June, when great swathes of the tall grass were cut and laid out to dry, sweetly smelling and wholesome. We piled it in heaps and jumped over it and into it with glee, then lay with our hands behind our head, watching the clouds scudding by, the farmer hoping they would not bring rain, no doubt. Aunt Edie would bring us out some lemonade and a piece of Gran's cake, then sit in the hay with us to share the feast. Life was good!

It was further to walk to Gran's, and we missed hopping over the stone stile to see her, but we soon got used to it and enjoyed the walk from one end of the Common to the other. The Common in springtime was a mass of yellow buttercups — creamy yellow shiny buttercups, each opening their shiny waistcoats with pride to the sun, the pollen from their stamens covering the toecaps of my shoes. There was a well-trodden path through the grass; to the right was a steep-sided field aptly called the Hilly Ground, which was great in wintertime if snow fell, for tobogganing, providing you steered clear of the old oak tree halfway down the hill. To the left were the large, set back houses of the gentry bordering the old coach road which separated the surrounds of their estates from the Common. A little further down was the Quaker meeting house and burial ground, and opposite was the village hall, the ground for its construction was given by Mrs Tuckett, who owned most of the land in Frenchay, it had a stage and kitchen, a good dance floor, and was the centre of our community for social events — WI, British Legion, Mothers' Union, Girls' Friendly Society, whist drives, shows, plays for the stage, barn dances and Old Time dances. The floor for dancing was specially made and considered excellent, and carefully looked after. I seem to remember it was sprinkled with powdered chalk before a dance. I know it was great to slide on, but the grown-ups soon stopped that game.

I started school at five years of age, in the Church of England School on the Common at Frenchay and near the church. The Common was out of bounds during school time. The classroom was one large room, which could be separated by a partition on rollers to separate the two different age groups attending the school. I can't remember much else about it, except the horrible toilets of the time. For some reason I then transferred to Whiteshill School when I was seven. I caught the bus on the coach road, which dropped me off at Whiteshill Common, opposite the school. After school, I walked home to Frenchay, which was about half an hour's walk around the road, or slightly less across the fields. I think the bus fare was a halfpenny, but in winter Mum would give me a penny to catch the bus home in the afternoon, if the weather was bad. If it was not too bad, I would follow the road back, where there was a little baker's shop, which sold big, plump currant buns for a halfpenny. The walk back through the fields was slightly shorter and quite pleasant except for a dark wooded dell, where the path led after leaving the road. I always scuttled through there pretty fast, and was always glad to be out in the open field again.

Gran's bungalow lay where the fields ended, and the Common began, by Becks Pool. I usually called in on my way home from school, and Gran would ask me if I was hungry — the answer was always yes! Gran would say, 'There's some bread and beef dripping in the larder, and you know where the treacle is,' (the treacle was actually Golden Syrup in a tin.) There was always a basin of beef dripping at Gran's. A beef dripping sandwich and treacle is lovely — try it! But there again, perhaps not, beef dripping is not the same today. Gran's was soft and spreadable. I wouldn't like you to be disappointed.

Esme had rheumatic fever when she was quite young, and was ill in bed for several months. The treatment was complete warmth and in those days eight aspirin a day. After a month of this treatment, she was sent to a children's convalescent hospital near Torquay, where Mum had to leave her at the hospital front door, into the care of the matron. Esme cried bitterly, she had been given a new teddy bear by Dad, but it was taken away from her straight away. Visiting time was once a month. This was not a happy house, as you might guess. Mum was never very strong and tired easily, but her tremendous spirit did not let her give in; she was prescribed raw, chopped-up liver to eat every day. The cause of her tiredness was diagnosed several years later — it was pernicious anaemia. In previous years, she would have died from it, but a cure had been found. It was due to the lack of vitamin B12, which her liver was not producing. From then on, vitamin B12 was given by injection once a month. In later years, twice a month.

There was a great moment when Dad made a crystal wireless set; it was a big day. I think we had to use headphones but it was still magic. We already had a gramophone, with a large horn where the sound came from — His Master's Voice. We had many good records of the time. Mum would sing along with them, Dad and I would sing along to 'Yip I addy I ay I ay' and my favourite, 'Lily of Laguna'.

During the summer holidays, the young children from boarding school came home to their parents or grandparents at Frenchay. Jeremy was the youngest son of the Cecil Frys, a few years younger than me, but I was often asked to go down to Riverwood during the holidays to keep him company for a few hours in the morning. The grounds of the house were quite spacious with plenty of shrubs for hide-and-seek and ball games on the lawn. There was quite a lot of running about — Granfer caught us running through the greenhouses and shouted out, 'You must not run through the greenhouses,' which was quite right, of course, but he picked us a bunch of ripe grapes to share. Cook would give us a small snack in the kitchen mid-morning. Monica Fry, the daughter of the McGreggor Frys, had a small cycle similar to mine, good for cycling round their circular drive, we belonged to the same Brownie pack, which was held in a room adjoining their house, The Cedars.

Mrs Tanner's granddaughter came to stay for a week or two at Frenchay. The Tanner's house was almost opposite Gran's bungalow and called Manor House. Her granddaughter and I were both interested in butterflies and insects; their garden was ideal hunting ground, and armed with butterfly nets, jam jars with brown paper covers tied with string and small holes pricked in the top, we collected quite a few, which, after naming them from a nature book, we let go free. It always seemed to be sunny then.

Mr Curry looked after their garden. He lived in a house across the cobbled yard. He had a son called Harold, much older than me, who collected foreign stamps, which was also one of my hobbies. I remember timidly knocking on their door one day. 'Please would Harold have any foreign stamps spare and as swaps?' Spare and swaps is stamp collectors' talk. I didn't hear anything from Harold, I expect he thought, 'Silly girl!'

Mrs Fry would give a Christmas party for Gran, Aunt Edie, Mum, Esme and me. There was a nice tea laid out for us in the dining room, and a present for each of us. I still have the necklace she gave me. Afterwards Mr Fry gave a cinematograph show with a Felix the cat cartoon — it was magic.

8

There was a cult in the medical world at that time that if a child had a sore throat on several occasions, the remedy was to take their tonsils and adenoids out. There was a special day of the week for this; the nurses referred to it as 'Blood Bath Day'. Dr Crossman, the doctor for Frenchay and Hambrook, decided that Esme and I should have this done on the same day. The day arrived. Mum, Esme and I arrived at the hospital. Esme was taken away first, then it was my turn for the stretcher. I remember being told to blow up a ball or balloon. I took a deep breath, and there was a horrible smell — which I now know was ether — and my head went round and round as if I was on a gramophone turntable. The next thing I remember is waking up, lying on the floor with a prickly blanket over me. I was in a long line of children, all lying on the floor, some crying, some being sick. I just lay there. Mum had been given a time to collect us and take us home. Mrs Fry had sent the Rolls, driven by Jack, the chauffeur, to bring us home. Mum, Esme and I sat in the voluminous back seat of the Rolls, our little bottoms sliding about in the spaciousness. As we glided through the outskirts of Bristol, Esme said she felt sick — too late! She was sick on the back seat. Fortunately, Mum had caught most of it in a towel, but she was terribly embarrassed. Jack said never mind, but I expect he did; driving the Rolls and keeping it in tip-top condition was his pride and joy, his other job was helping Granfer in the garden, but he wasn't very interested in that. We had ice cream for tea. I don't know where it had come from, but it was bliss to our sore throats. Esme recovered quickly and wanted something to eat immediately, but I couldn't eat for several days.

Nineteen-twenty-eight was an eventful year. Mum told us we were moving to another house, up towards the church and the Common. I didn't want to leave my familiar surroundings. I woke early on the day we moved and gazed out of the window of my little world. I was sorry to leave my little bedroom and said so in my mind as I stroked the familiar walls. But times move on and I cautiously welcomed our new house and home; it was called Rose Cottage.

Chapter 3

Rose Cottage

There was a lovely view from the front of our new home, quite unusually so, as you were looking across a valley to the fields beyond, over the tops of tall trees. At the bottom of this deep valley was the River Frome. Quarrying in the past had gouged out sections of the rock base, so it was almost like viewing from a cliff top. Quarrying was still continuing further over on the Downend side of the valley, there was a faint murmur from the distant machinery, but scarcely noticeable, and in a year the quarries finished altogether.

There were three bedrooms and three downstairs rooms, one was used as a large kitchen with a kitchen range. We had most of our meals here, around a large gate-leg table with sides that dropped down. The room was always warm night and day, as the fire to support it was always kept in. It had to be black-leaded once a week, which was a drawback, and it was eventually replaced by a cream-coloured modern range, also kept in all the time in the winter by keeping the fire going, it was coal fired. Attached to the kitchen was an 'outhouse'. When we first went there it was approached by an outside door, which meant going out of the kitchen door and re-entering the outhouse side door. Eventually a door was made directly from the kitchen. The outhouse had a stone built copper, which was lit by a coal fire underneath it, this was where the clothes were washed and boiled once a week, a large bleached white copper stick stirred the washing, and enabled the washing to be removed from the copper. Our mangle had huge rollers for putting the rinsed washing through, to squeeze as much water out as possible. I was allowed to turn the mangle when I was home during school holidays, but the heavy cotton sheets proved a bit too much for me.

Best of all, we had electricity, not elaborate but good after candles and oil lamps.. The coal was kept in the cellar, which was a large underground room with a stone-flagged floor. The entrance to it was through a wooden door in the hall at the bottom of the stairs, which led to stone stairs or steps down to the cellar. There was a very low wattage electric light, which made it feel quite eerie. Coal was delivered through a large paving stone hole, in the paved area at the side of the house, which, when not in use, was covered by a thick piece of wood as a lid. The coalman called at regular times with a ton of coal. Each hundred-weight would shoot into the cellar with a thud and a crunch, sometimes huge blocks, which eventually had to be broken down with a coal hammer when required to fill the coal scuttle. If I was at home and the coalman was coming, my job was to count the bags as they were delivered down the hole, all 20 bags of them. It's very easy to daydream when you are doing that, but I could nip out and count the empty bags, which were supposed to be laid on the ground by the hole each delivery. It didn't do any harm to be 'on the watch', as a cwt of coal was worth quite a bit, and money was short in those days.

There were sash windows in all the downstairs rooms and quite unusually, wooden shutters, which folded back into the side of the window frame, which was very useful in the Second World War in later years. Mum and Dad set to work in getting the garden straight, which was very overgrown; they loved gardening, and so do Esme and I. We each had our own bit of garden, which we encircled with stones, stating ownership.

The soil was quite poor all over the garden, the fine particles quickly allowed the nutrients to drain away when it rained, the moisture then filtered away through the rocks below and eventually down to the river level. The soil improved greatly over the years with compost and manure. I remember we had several bags of 'spent mushroom' compost delivered where it was lain over the ground, and hey presto! suddenly one morning a marvellous crop of mushrooms appeared.

The front of the house was covered with ivy, plus one solitary white climbing rose, which magically seemed to grow from a small patch of earth between the paving stones at the side of the house. It grew right up to the bedroom window and had the most marvellous perfume; it was a pleasure to open the bedroom window in the morning. The rampant ivy was host to hundreds of woodlice, we called them 'woodlyice'. They had to be removed when the ivy was stripped off, which was a job for Esme and I, brush and pan was our best plan; if you touch a crawling woodlice it will curl up into a ball, and then it's easy to scoop it up into a bucket, which is what we did. We took the half-filled bucket to the bottom of the garden and tipped them over the wall, where there was a long drop down to the bushes below. I don't think they minded the long drop down, but they may have had a bit of a headache!

Christmas was always great fun. On Christmas Eve, Dad would take me into Bristol on the bus, a great treat in itself, to see all the lights and shops, with so much to sell in them, and so many people. It was my twice-a-year trip out of the village. In the summer, there was the annual Sunday School day trip to Weston-super-Mare by Charabanc from Frenchay Common, and Christmas Eve with Dad. It was magic. There were lots of strange parcels under his arm as the evening went on, and a special cake he had to collect from his place of work. It was a wonder world of marzipan animals, sugar pigs, decorations, Christmas trees, carol singers, all shops open selling their wares, and lights, lights everywhere! What a sight for my eyes, and to cap it all Dad took me into a shop or café — could it have been Melhuises? — where we sat at a small table and Dad bought me a two-coloured ice cream in a dish! It was dark when we got home, I don't think it was late, but Esme and I were off to bed, having left our letter for Father Christmas.

Some older girls had told me there was no Father Christmas, and that it was my dad. I decided to stay awake to see Father Christmas. I waited and waited and listened. There was some movement from the stairs, and a rustling, of paper perhaps? Deep breathing, then a loud exclamation. I carefully opened one eye — Father Christmas had got stuck in the bedroom door trying to get himself and two bulging pillowcases through the door. I think he had overdone the Christmas Eve bottle of sherry. I closed my eye quickly, smiled to myself and dropped off to sleep. Your secret is safe with me Father Christmas

On Christmas morning we all went down to Gran's for the day, taking our presents in my doll's pram to show Gran. Gran would be in the kitchen with her face flushed and beads of perspiration on her forehead, as she spooned the fat over the glistening turkey, it would only just fit into the oven, the Frys always gave them a lovely turkey at Christmas. Granfer would be in his best clothes, smoking his pipe and sitting in his special chair. Aunt Edie had a little smile on her face, we knew she always had a little surprise for us all at teatime. Christmas dinner was perfection, Christmas pudding made by Gran months earlier was brought in with the flaming ceremony, telltale indentations on the side assured us children of a silver thrupenny piece. In the afternoon we played snakes and ladders and 'sevens' with Aunt Edie and the playing cards — Snap was a little too loud for the afternoon as the 'grown ups' were having forty winks, in other words a little nap. There was iced Christmas cake for tea and an iced sponge cake that had been specially made for us, Aunt Edie came in with a furled umbrella, when she opened it, there was a little present for everyone, each one tied to the spoke of the umbrella. Granfer played his concertina in the evening and some old gramophone records that we had heard many times before, but it was great and Granfer could sing very well. There were more games in the evening, very loud snap, and I-spy with my little eye, then it was off to bed for us two children, in Aunt Edie's bedroom. I had the camp bed and Esme slept with Aunt Edie in her bed. Mum and Dad went home in the evening. The next day Gran, Granfer and Aunt Edie came up to Rose Cottage for dinner, Dad and Granfer went to watch the local football match on the Common, played every Boxing Day morning.

The tranquillity of it all I can feel, even now.

In the Spring Esme and I went to dancing lessons at Miss Eardley's at Staplehill. It was half an hour's walk, but no one seemed to mind in those days, and we enjoyed it. In the summertime, we were part of a dancing display, held on the stage at the Vandyke Cinema, Fishponds.

I had a solo dance, The Scottish Reel, complete with sporran, and crossed imitation swords on the floor. Esme was a 'mushroom' in a group of five other little girls, the outfits were expensive, the best pink velvet for the mushroom, and authentic tartan long socks for me. Fortunately, Mum was good at sewing and in fact could make something out of anything, nevertheless, dancing displays were a very expensive business, as, by what I hear, they are today.

I made some good friends at Whiteshill School, where I moved to when I was seven years old. I can picture them now, even though the names escape me. Hmmm… Joan Stallard… Yes, Frank Palmer, his father was the headmaster and a very good teacher, I owe a lot to him. Harvey Bready? Three out of ten? I must try harder! Most of the children lived quite near and went home to lunch but I had to take sandwiches, we were not allowed in the school during the lunch hour, and so in the summer I ate my sandwiches on the Common. If it was wet or cold, I went to a large covered space underneath the school, it was damp and dark and open-fronted to the wind, it was where games were carried out in wet weather. The floor was asphalted and no one was supposed to go down there outside of lesson time, but where else was I supposed to go?

My time at Whiteshill School was coming to an end, I had enjoyed it very much, but it was 1931 and time for me to take the 11+ exam, for either Chipping Sodbury or Kingswood Grammar School. It didn't worry me a bit. I remember Mr Palmer, the headmaster, calling me into his office some weeks later to say I had done well, and had gained a scholarship to Kingswood Grammar School, at the time there were very few of these on offer as they were fee-paying schools. Mr Palmer gave me a long envelope to give to my parents, and I almost flew home. Yes, I did catch the bus home that day.

Mum and Dad were pleased, but the possible cost of the uniform, sports equipment, transport etc, tempered their excitement a little. As you can imagine, for a fee-paying school, it was nothing but the best — shantung summer dresses, real Panama hats, hockey sticks and gym equipment. Dad had a steady job at Willways, where he kept the books for Mr Willway, he had the most excellent handwriting and was well thought of by Mr Willway. The pay was £3.50 a week, an average for the times I think. It was the 1930s and the time of the Great Depression.

Bristol Aeroplane Company was expanding, making engines for the Blenheim. The wages were good and many men were taking jobs there, but at the time, the thinking was that it could not last, but of course it did. Dad remained loyal to Willways and his steady job and never regretted it, except at this particular time, when the extra money would have been very useful, but I respect him for that. Loyalty comes high on our family creed. Willways expanded and he became their secretary.

There was a coach that collected pupils from the surrounding area to take them to Kingswood School, it would pick me up in the morning, and bring me back in the afternoon, it was about half an hour's ride. There was no other way of getting to the school from Frenchay. It cost £5 a term, which was quite a lot of money then, Dad agreed to pay it himself.

The winter uniform was a chocolate brown gymslip, cream shirt, and a brown velour hat with a pale blue band and the school emblem on the front, and a chocolate brown blazer, with the blue school crest on the pocket. To save the expense of the shop prices, Mum made the gymslip, shirts and dresses, but the blazer had to be bought plus hockey stick, tennis racquet and press plus PE kit and plimsolls — then I was complete and ready for school. Thus I walked down the Common on my first morning, to wait for the coach that would take me on my new venture.

Kingswood Grammar School seemed daunting at first glance, seemingly hundreds of children being disgorged from dozens of coaches, the equivalent of today's 'parent depositing' by private car. New entrants were assigned classrooms after morning assembly, and an individual peg in the cloakroom, for outdoor clothes and PE bag. The list of subjects to be taken and the classroom for each were displayed in an alcove just off of the corridor, which stretched the length of the school, with classrooms and laboratories on either side.

The list of subjects to be taken was quite mind stretching, but exciting, and I took to the new subjects well. I loved biology, art, geography and geometry in particular.

There was a tuck shop that opened after the midday break. Pocket money was not in my vocabulary, although most of the other girls seemed to have some, but that didn't bother me.

I loved hockey and all the other outdoor sports, it was the opening of new horizons, new subjects, and new knowledge; everything was fine and I was doing well.

In the second year, in the high jump on sports day, I landed heavily on the front of my right toe. There was no apparent damage done, but the movement of the big toe joint became very painful. An appointment was made for the removal of the joint by Mr Chitty at the BRI. The foot and leg were in plaster for two weeks, and when the plaster was removed, the toe was infected and inflamed. The foot exercises that should have followed were not possible and the process eventually took six weeks to clear up, but, more importantly, the big toe had set immovably. Going back to school I had lost track in the lessons I had missed, and I struggled to catch up, I did to a certain degree, but I did worry and began to get dulling migraines, distorted vision, and numb, tingling hands and tongue, which always meant being sent to 'sick bay' rest room for the rest of the day.

Mrs Fry always insisted that Mrs Mann kept her informed on what happened to Mum, Esme and myself, and the outcome of this particular happening was that she arranged for Mr Chitty, the surgeon who did the operation, to come to her house at Frenchay, to meet me in her drawing room, to see what could be done for me. After removing my shoes and socks, Mr Chitty asked me to run barefoot across the lawn, whilst he watched the movement of my foot.

He said that nothing could be done, the big toe would have to be removed. I couldn't bear the thought of this, and told him so, he was not too pleased and replied that I would have to have special shoes made for me, with a wooden bar across the sole. I was mortified. Mrs Fry had the shoes specially made for me in Park Street, they were black lace-ups, with a wooden bar right across the sole, and highly expensive. I was very grateful to Mrs Fry and her interest in me, but I felt miserable and ugly wearing them, every step was a rocking movement in these special shoes. I did try, but I found it impossible in everyday use, as my whole gait was altered, I returned to my own shoes. To this day my toe is as rigid as ever, and my foot has assumed a funny shape, but I live with it, every pair of shoes I buy take on an odd shape after a short while.

Dancing lessons had to stop, as they became an extra expense on the family budget, but there was the social side to the village that filled in the spare times in life — a tennis and bowls club was started in the grounds of the Miss Surtees, a very pleasant place, with grass courts and a very presentable bowling green, where Dad played (I still have his own special bowls) and I played tennis.

Every week Gran would leave a message in the summer for me to come down and mow her lawn. I always enjoyed doing this, Aunt Edie would cut the edges of the lawn with shears, and I managed the lawn mower. Lawn mowers in those times were quite small, and physically pushed, not like today's monsters. Job finished, I would have some tea with Gran, and as I left, she would always press something in my hand — it was a silver sixpence; she always insisted I took it, however much I said I was only too pleased to do it for her. It went in a little box at home, and was saved up for Christmas presents.

I had made some good friends at school — Eunice and Renee lived at Downend, and would come to tea occasionally, the favourite sandwiches were banana and apricot jam spread — it's funny how you remember simple little things.

For a while I had school dinners, which were 2/6 a week. An older student, a prefect, came around the classrooms to collect dinner money on a Monday, she overlooked me one Monday, and I tried to find her, to give it to her, but all the older girls looked the same to me, and as younger ones, we were rather in awe of them. We changed classrooms for almost every lesson, carrying our books in a satchel. I did try to tell one teacher. He gave me the name of a prefect, but I had no idea where to find her. By Friday the 2/6 was still in my pocket, and I bought some chocolate biscuits from the tuck shop. I still feel guilty about that, and have been scrupulously honest ever since in everything I do. Soon afterwards I stopped school dinners — I didn't want that problem again. Mum cooked for us when Dad came home in the evening and I took sandwiches for lunch, which were allowed, you just sat at a different table.

Mum took plenty of interest in the social life of the village, especially in the British Legion. She ran jumble sales for the Legion funds. All the clothes given were collected and sorted in our end room with the help of other members. Trestle tables were put up around the top lawn, two o'clock was opening time, and a good time was had by all. Quite a good sum was raised for this good cause and everyone gave generously. Times were hard in the '30s, and a good jumble sale was appreciated.

Mum was also on the committee of the WI. Each member was asked in their turn to make the cakes for refreshment time at the next WI meeting.

Mum was always outspoken, and said she didn't think it was right to expect committee members to have to meet all the cost as many of them couldn't afford it. Gran was very displeased with Mum over this, I expect because Mrs Fry was on the committee also.

Aunt Edie, as I have said before, was very deaf from an early age, and her sight slightly impaired, although her sisters helped her with speech and reading by forming the words with their lips, which she would copy. There were four other sisters, Edith, Ada, Lily, Hilda and Mum, who was called May, she was the youngest. When Aunt Edie was twelve years old she went to a school for the deaf and partially sighted in Bristol, where she was taught a form of Braille. Pupils were not usually accepted at the school after the age of 10 years, so I don't know how that was arranged. The school was run as a charitable school and supported by money from the wealthy of Bristol, including the Quakers who were a prominent, benevolent part of the Bristol community. Aunt Edie was there for two years, which was to prove a blessing to her, for as Granfer was chopping some wood a splinter flew into her eye, it was removed at the eye infirmary, but the sight was lost in that eye and over the following years the eyes deteriorated until everything was a shadow, but the Braille library books were a great comfort to her and Mum continued to help her with her pronunciation whilst she still had some sight.

At school my reports were good, and I had caught up on my missing six weeks. Art was my joy, it all came so easily to me, and I always got very good marks, but I thought being there was proving too much for the family. Mum was not well, Esme was not strong after her long illness, and the situation hung heavily on my mind. I had another year to complete my schooling, and I liked it very much. I made a decision during the summer holidays — I was not going back to school. Telling my parents was not easy. Quite naturally they were furious with me for what was, to them, wasted years, money, and opportunities. I had no answers. They were right in their condemnation. I withdrew into myself.

Chapter 4

I awoke the next morning, relieved the decision had been made but feeling strangely empty and flat — who was I, what was I? I knew I had to prove myself to my parents and myself. I felt, contrary to my parents' belief, that my past education had not been wasted, there was another world outside of Frenchay, and Kingswood School had given me an insight and a feeling to investigate and continue the learning process. I looked at all the possibilities to get me started in the local paper, BT were offering switchboard training, I applied and was accepted, so began an interesting time, eventually moving to a large switchboard with a private company.

Home life was more settled, and importantly to me, I was able to contribute. I cycled to work, which was the other side of Bristol, about six miles from Frenchay. One evening a week I went roller skating near the Downs, and from there progressed to ice skating at the rink in Bristol, I loved that! I had white ice skating boots and a black satin skating skirt. Living so far out of town, transport was quite difficult. Mum always insisted on me being home by ten o'clock, and would be waiting up for me if I was a bit late. Looking back, it was understandable, as there wasn't a bus service later at night and my bicycle was my only means of transport. Cycle lamps were pretty dim, especially if the battery was getting low, and there were no street lamps after Beech Hill, Stapleton, which meant another two miles of unlit country road to Frenchay, before reaching home.

One day I came home to find Mum had been taken to Hambrook Hospital; she had had a stroke and had lost the use of her right leg and her speech was slightly impaired. Matron said she would never walk again. Esme went to stay with Gran. Dad spent every evening at the hospital with Mum. Mum vowed that she would walk again, she had a tremendous spirit, we could only hope.

At age 40, it was quite young to have a stroke. Dad was glad I was at home, he was more likely to cook for two than just himself, and I did what I could. Dad was quite interested in cooking, which I think he had acquired from his mother. One day he made a rabbit stew, and for a joke put some currants in the gravy, feigning surprise and shock when dishing it out — for a brief moment I fell for that one! Gran did all our washing, and so it was we managed and were able to visit Mum every night. Her speech was improving.

One evening, after visiting Mum and calling on Gran and Esme, Dad and I were walking back home. I can see the spot quite clearly in my mind even now, where Dad said to me, 'Gran is not your real gran.' I was quite taken aback, and said, 'Who is then?' Dad replied that he did not know. I said, 'Who is my grandfather?' he replied that all he knew was that my grandfather was an artist who travelled abroad a lot, and that Gran was paid 10 shillings a week for fostering and looking after Mum. Gran kept her knowledge strictly to herself. At this point Dad changed the subject, perhaps thinking he had said too much, but I don't think at the time he knew any more. The moment passed and it was many years later before it began to enter my head again — such are the pressing priorities of the teenage mind.

Mum was in hospital for many weeks before being well enough to come home, determination had won her through, but her thick strong brown hair had turned white in the process. We were back as a family again.

My evenings at home were mostly spent knitting, doing embroidery, reading, and listening to the wireless. I wasn't much interested in boys, although they seemed more interesting as mates than girls. I had on order two monthly magazines — *The Geographical Magazine*, which inspired my desire to travel, and *Health and Strength*, which was my physical Guru. I exercised every night and loved the great outdoors, became a vegetarian, and drank only water. From my Brownie Box Camera and with help from my magazine, I learnt how to develop my own photographs.

Reading was a real pleasure — I belonged to a private lending library. The books were tuppence a book for two weeks, and were changed frequently. I liked travel, historical stories, autobiographies and biographies, but NOT Fiction.

Cycling was my ticket to the world beyond Frenchay. At 17, I decided to cycle from Frenchay to London, to visit my two aunts at Woodford Green and Romford, Essex. I left home at 4am with sandwiches, water and some chocolate in my saddlebag. My plan was to rest five minutes in every hour. Arthur, my Romford cousin, also a cyclist, arranged by letter (no phones!) to meet where my road to London joins the circular road around London. I said I would be there about 2.30pm — does that seem optimistic now? Well, I WAS there, pretty much on time, and Arthur guided me to Aunty Hilda's at Woodford Green. The next day we cycled to Romford and Aunty Lily's about 10 miles away where we had a good game of cricket with my other cousins in an adjacent field before returning to Woodford Green. The next morning I left for home at 8am for a distance of about 120 miles. By the time I got to Marshfield I was slowing down and wondering if I was going to make it home, it was mainly lack of 'fuel' (food), my legs had lost their stuffing, there were very few shops, if any, and it was past closing time, but I did find a small newsagents that could offer me some chocolate, and a glass of milk from their own kitchen. Oddly enough, that glass of milk was the best I've ever tasted, it put fresh life into my legs, and I was on my way again, arriving home about ten o'clock. Not bad for a three-speed Raleigh bike.

Blacks camping catalogue was a magnet for my thoughts. I knew the catalogue from end to end, and soon acquired from them a tent, a ground sheet (they were not built in like they are now), Primus stove, sleeping bag, integral knife, fork and spoon, a set of lightweight pans for easy packing, and a metal gripit for removing the pans from the stove when they were hot. I was ready to go camping, after first putting the tent up on the back lawn — but where?

I advertised in the local Bristol paper for a girl companion to join me on a week's cycling tour from Bristol, covering the North Coast of Devon. I had a reply from a girl who had been camping with her family, but not on her own. We were both 17.

I loaded the tent and equipment on my bicycle, my companion carried the groundsheet. My tent was comparatively lightweight cotton in those days, and the traditional shape, but the great thing was the zipped entrance that ran from eaves to ground, not the usual tape ties — 'Blacks' first! I was very proud of it. From the beginning, it was clear my companion had never camped on her own, and didn't have much idea about DIY camping; it had been her dad's idea to reply to my advert.

Our first night's stop was in a farmer's field, with his permission, just outside of Bridgwater. It was drizzling a bit, but we brewed up and boiled some eggs, then retired into our sleeping bags.

The next morning was brighter, and it was on the road to Minehead and some photographs on the sea wall for the record with my Box Brownie camera, after that, via Porlock Hill to Lynton, then came some dry weather with reasonable campsites, and so onwards, the Valley of Rocks and Clovelly, where we had to make the decision to turn around and make for home along much the same route we had come. I think our main meals were cheese, tomatoes, bread and butter and Marmite — it was tough, and I enjoyed the challenge, but I think my companion was glad to be going home.

Every available summer evening I sat out in the garden to eat my meals, with Mum's six hens roaming around to keep me company, being a vegetarian, cheese was my main protein, with plenty of vegetables. I was probably a complete 'pain in the derrière', but life was interesting and full of things to explore.

I had tea with my Gran, Dad's mother occasionally, she would tell me of her sister who emigrated to Canada and married there, where they established a camp on the shores of Lake Ontario, of log cabins. She gave me a brochure, which fired my enthusiasm. I would work my passage on a boat — I wrote to several shipping companies, and made a list of what I would take with me. I had a reply, Mum was curious about the envelope, and that was the end of that. Mum said I was secretive, I suppose I was, but I think everything is possible, but then other people tell you you can't do it. I must have been a strange child. I lived with my thoughts and still do. Cycling satisfies my feeling of restlessness inside, creates the exhilaration you get when you feel you could move a mountain, run like the wind to exhaustion, then throw yourself on a grassy bank, and sleep with nature and the good earth.

I loved music; there was a musical instrument shop in the Bristol Arcade which I gazed in often. There was a shiny blue mottled accordion that I coveted very much. It was £20 and way out of my reach. I could only look. One day when the sight of it became too much, I asked Dad if he would agree to sign an agrement, and I would repay him in 12 months — hire purchase in other words, which was not considered in our house; Mum was horrified at the thought of this — you didn't buy unless you had the money to pay for it — full stop. Dad came from a musical family and had learnt the piano in his younger days. I think his mother may have helped him come to a decision, but he bought the accordion for me, and I repaid him every month for 12 months. Accordions are quite loud instruments so I practised in our end room, some distance from the family. I managed quite well, my favourite tune was *South of the Border*. Mum was quite pleased in a way, as she loved music and singing, and I was quite pleased to pay Dad in good time; mind you, I didn't have a penny to bless myself with for that year, but who cares — money isn't everything.

In my work as switchboard operator, I had my own little room and during my lunch hour I was thumbing through my Black's catalogue when my colleague came in and said 'Why don't you join the CTC Camping Section (Cyclist Touring Club), I can give you the address of the secretary, they go out camping every weekend in the summer, and there are Sunday day runs every other week in the winter.' I was interested immediately and wrote away for details. The secretary replied to say I would be very welcome, and the next meet was at Chewton Mendip, the rest of the club would be at the start of the 'meet' at the top of Brislington Hill, on the outskirts of Bristol, at 11am. I would be there! Amazingly, everything for camping was packed inside and outside of my saddlebag, including a small Hovis loaf, a full butter dish, the indispensable jar of Marmite, and camping cutlery. My enamel mug hung on the saddlebag side pocket. The tent and groundsheet, plus my sleeping bag, packed in a waterproof bag, was strapped onto the top of my saddlebag. I must have looked like a travelling gypsy. I had a neat, blue elastic waist belt, with two small zipped pockets to carry some spare money. Loaded up, off I went. I learnt afterwards that Mum had thought I had left my purse behind and would be without money, so poor Dad was sent off on his bike to try and catch me up, but of course I had a head start and he gave up the chase at Stapleton.

It was quite a steep hill to the start of the meet, where I found a motley crowd of about 12 cyclists were waiting. There were four girls and eight boys, aged about 25-30, all quite a bit older than me; this included two married cyclist couples. There must have been a few smiles at my gear! Big mistake on my part was a flock sleeping bag — much too bulky! Primus stove still in its original tin box — oh dear! Good thinking to keep the smell of paraffin away from the Hovis, but a very awkward shape in the saddlebag. I learnt a lot in the course of the weekend. Number one — all seasoned cycle campers braise on the Primus stove to the cycle tubing, but in a few weeks someone had done that for me. Number two — I had bought some blue suitable material and a pound of goose down feathers (a pound-and-a-half would have been better) and Jack Turner made a sleeping bag on his mother's sewing machine. He used to make his own tent every spring and in the autumn's last meet, set fire to it, and we all danced round it like Indians! Quite an unorthodox bunch, but great fun. The new sleeping bag was light and warm, and packed down to less than half the size of the kapok one; every ounce counts when you are cycle camping. I was learning fast.

The campsites were always on a farm; many favourites that were returned to every year. They were all very basic, but we were always welcomed. Milk and eggs were collected from the farm. We played cricket every weekend, the bat was a suitable piece of wood from the hedge. We went for walks, had campfires in the evening, with the farmer's permission, and we were careful to put the turf back afterwards, and always left the campsite as we had found it.

We played skittles with the locals on a Saturday night in the village pub, and walked back to the campsite by the light of the moon singing camp songs quietly — nothing rowdy. I remember one lad who sang *The Red Flag*, which was just the right tempo for marching it was all quite harmless and good fun, we were at peace with the world and in the company of myriads of glow worms that glowed in the hedgerows that night. A whole weekend would cost us less than a shilling.

One couple I met on my first meet was 'Ging' and Harry Crap. On the Sunday afternoon, as we 'made up' camp to go home, they asked me if I thought my parents might like to meet them, to see what kind of folk I was going camping with, and what our Club was like. They said they would be going my way home as they lived at Stapleton, and would like to call in with me. I accepted gladly, and they got on very well with Mum and Dad, especially as Harry Craps' brother played cricket for Gloucester County, and you know how much Dad liked cricket! It was very thoughtful of them, and this applied to all members of the camping club CTC — dedicated cyclists who were always willing to help.

Compared with the other club cyclists, my bicycle — although a three-speed — was the 'sit up and beg' type; a very good friend and still giving good service, but I had seen a lovely top-of-the-range Raleigh touring bicycle in a cycle shop window. It was blue with white Bluemel mudguards and a new type gear change with Sturmey Archer five-speed handlebar-trigger-controlled gears. I passed the shop every day on my way home. During the week I had to make a difficult decision to sell my beloved accordion to buy the bicycle, for about the same price. With regret, I sold my accordion, but vowed to get another one in the future when I was wealthier. I bought the bicycle and a white saddlebag to complete the picture. I felt like the 'bee's knees' — as the saying was at the time.

One of the oldest members of the club was Len Norman. His nephew at the time was a lone cyclist, and his uncle asked him if he would like to come out to our next campsite, which he did, and from then on became a regular camper, sharing his uncle's quite large tent. Looking back from present times, it seems like another world — of genuine friendship, peace, and simple pleasures. And so it was.

Building up to July and August, on the political front, storm clouds were gathering. Volunteers were asked to join the Civil Nursing Reserve, I joined. The training was one night a week at a centre in Bristol. I was always very interested in nursing and things medical, and found the lessons informative and worthwhile. After the course, 20 hours had to be spent assisting at the Bristol Royal Infirmary, including night duty and all aspects of nursing, including A&E.

Camping and cycling continued during August. I took Esme on a camping holiday to Christchurch near Bournemouth. I cycled there with all the camping gear, leaving home later than intended, having a problem with my gears — not a good idea, and it was getting dark. When I was nearly there, there was a terrible thunderstorm and vivid lightning, I thought the lightning might strike my metal handlebars and me, and Mum would wonder what I was doing cycling through the night, so I took shelter in a barn just off of the road, where there were some straw bales. I did think about making a cup of powdered soup on the Primus, but then — no way! There was too much straw around. Then something rustled in the straw — a rat, I think. The storm faded, and I was on my way, arriving at the campsite in the early morning.

The campsite was in semi-darkness, but I found an open space and put the tent up and crawled into my sleeping bag, meeting Esme off the coach from Bristol at mid day. It was a good week. Dad and our cousin Arthur, who was staying a few days with Gran, came down on a day trip to see us.

At the end of the week I saw Esme safely on the coach to Bristol and wandered back to the tent. Esme had her ticket in her pocket, and Dad was meeting her at the coach station in Bristol. Sitting quietly in my tent, I was shocked to see Esme walking back across the field, with her suitcase. It emerged that when asked for her ticket by the conductor when the coach was on the outskirts of Christchurch, she had forgotten where it was, couldn't show it, and the conductor/inspector had turned her off of the coach. She was 13! I calmed her down, and got in touch with Bristol coach station by phone, who put out a tannoy message for Dad to tell him Esme would be on the next coach. All ended well but it should never have happened. We had a sincere apology from the coach company and a refund. Come the September of 1939, after a happy year-and-a-half with my club friends, it all had to come to an end. War was declared with Germany. Life would change for us all.

Chapter 5

Our World as we knew it changed overnight in September 1939 when Germany invaded Poland and war was declared. Camping came to an end that weekend, and everyone's thoughts were, what could we do to help our country. As a Civil Nursing Reserve auxiliary, my services were not at that moment required. Those early days were sometimes called 'the phoney war' — in other words, nothing was apparently going on, but everyone was waiting apprehensively, keyed-up, and waiting for the first blow.

Len's nephew, Ken Norman, applied with another camper, to join the Tank Corps, but they were told to come back in a few months' time, as they had too many volunteers, for the time being. I was still finishing my quota of night duties at the Bristol Royal Infirmary for the Civil Nursing Reserve, from ward duties to casualty. I remember a badly injured motorcyclist being brought into a side ward in casualty, because of an air-raid alarm, we were on stand-by lighting. As the nearest nurse, a torch was handed to me to focus its strong beam onto the motorcyclist's injured head, whilst the casualty doctor tried to save him. I don't think the motorcyclist survived but when the doctor realised I was only a Nursing Reserve, he said I had done well.

I saw an advertisement in the Frenchay Post Office window — 'Join the ARP' (Air Raid Precautions). I applied to join, was accepted, and appointed to Bristol, Brislington section. We worked in shifts, day and night, manning the telephones, and in the event of an air-raid co-ordinated all the services involved. The 'blackout' came into existence from the beginning of the war, not a chink of light must be showing outside, car lights had shades over the top of them, to throw the light downwards, and the wood shutters of Rose Cottage came in very useful in this respect. Dad joined the Home Guard as soon as it was formed, and he was very much part of the British Legion, as he was also after the war. Mum ran jumble sales, trestle tables were arranged on the lawn, and our 'end room' became the sorting office for all the donated clothes. The platform of stone under the stairs, and leading to the cellars, was kept prepared with spare blankets, pillows, and some non-perishable food, as a place for us to go when the air-raid sirens went off.

By 1940 London had been bombed by the Luftwaffa (German bombers) and their raids spread to other major cities including Bristol. Ken applied to join the RAF and was accepted for Bomber Command. He did his basic training at Yatesbury.

I wanted to join the services, especially the WAAF, and pestered the recruitment offices, but I was told I was in a reserved occupation CNR. Shortly afterwards I received a call from the CNR to report to Frenchay Hospital, which had been designated a military hospital, to find it was to look after three wards of evacuee children, suffering from a range of infectious problems — measles, mumps and chicken pox. There was a staff nurse and two more CNRs to complete the team. The epidemic lasted about two months — long hours but rewarding. The poor little souls were far from home and often tearful. Gradually the epidemic waned and the children were settled in their new homes, and we were surplus to requirements.

Ken and I had become good friends, having plenty of things in common; we kept in touch regularly by letter, and met whenever he came home on leave and whatever time was available.

By 1941 he had passed all the required courses and was posted to Bomber Command Operational and took part in raids over Germany. He was allowed leave every six weeks, which was special to air crew, I believe, as there were no days off during the operational six weeks. Lord Nuffield gave all air crew an extra 2/6 a week, he also arranged hotel accommodation for overseas air crew in this country during their leave in Britain. Ken's station was RAF Waterbeach.

In the meantime, I had taken a telephone operator's job at Bristol Precision, a factory making cupolos for Wellington Bombers, the type of aircraft Ken was flying in, affectionately called 'Whimpys' by the RAF. On his fifth raid, his aircraft, loaded with bombs, had problems during take-off, the pilot had to manoeuvre the plane away from a nearby village and church spire, before crash-landing just outside of the village. All the crew escaped unhurt, but shaken.

One evening, as we walked home from the pictures at Fishponds, Ken said it was better if we didn't meet so much, many of his air crew friends were not returning from air-raids over Germany, and he didn't think it was fair to make promises to me. I felt sorry but agreed with his thoughts in principle, perhaps he had met someone else at Waterbeach — it was understandable for the times we were living in, when everyone lived for the moment. We parted friends, but I requested I walk home by myself, which I did. All letters ceased, and it was gloomy for a while, but once again I philosophically picked myself up and moved on.

Several weeks later I went down with yellow jaundice. I have heard since there was quite an epidemic in England at that time. Life was gloomy; I had to spend much time in bed, my diet was very limited, being devoid of fat of any kind — and no letters. Six long weeks and I was beginning to feel better. Then a knock came at the door, which Mum answered. It was Ken — he asked if he could see me. Mum asked him in, and so began our life story again, where it had left off.

Bristol Precision were very good to me when I returned to work, and when Ken was next home on leave, he was invited to a tour of the factory and to comment on any aspect of the manufacturing of the cupolas they were producing for the Wellington Bombers.

After many requests to the recruiting office, I was able to join the WAAF. Mum did not want me to go and said I didn't need to, as I was in a reserved occupation, but I think Dad was secretly pleased and proud of me, and I was delighted to be joining the services. Soon afterwards I was on my way. Dad came to see me off at Temple Meads Station, he had taken an hour off work to do so, then it was just me and the unknown.

RAF Hengistbury was where I was kitted out and my allotted course to follow in the WAAF was in signals section as a radio telephone operator.

All civilian clothes had to be sent home by post; the only place to get brown paper was the Naffi and it was so thin, but it had to do. My parcel arrived at home with half of my clothes hanging out, where my shoes had torn through the paper, the postman was amused, but Mum was NOT! Oh dear. After two weeks it was on to civvy billets at Morecombe and 'square bashing' for a month.

Morecombe in the winter is bleak and cold, and one morning inoculations were carried out on the top floor of a tall building, where a long, long line of us 'rookies' lined up, Indian file style, on the iron fire escape on the outside of the building. The queue snaked its way up to a large room, where we waited patiently until it was our turn for the needle, and several different types of inoculations. Then it was down to an empty cinema for more instruction, and we were assembled in squads, for 'square bashing' on the seafront promenade. It was a very, very, cold time. My service shoes were not yet broken in, my chilblains crucified me, and my inoculations in those following weeks had taken rather too well, which was very obvious to me when the standard command came 'Swing those arms' as we marched along the bitterly cold promenade of Morecombe, but I was still proud to be in the WAAF. Square bashing over, I was posted to RAF Cranwell, signals section on a RT (radio telephone) course of six weeks.

We were billeted in ex-married quarters. It was February and still bitterly cold. There were three blankets to a bed — grey, and with the feel of soft cardboard, one to place over the mattress, the other two to cover yourself with. The mattresses were in three sections, which were called biscuits. These had to be stacked at the base of the bed with the folded blankets on top every day when the call came to get up. I remember always being hungry there. Gran sent me a parcel, which included a Lyons swiss roll, I sat on my bed and ate it all in one sitting when there was no one around, although I am normally very good at sharing.

The time passed, my course was completed successfully and I was posted to Aston Down RAF station, near Stroud. Here we were in service huts, with one combustion stove in the middle of the hut. Lucky you if your bed was near the stove in the wintertime, but that did have its drawbacks, in 'off duty' time, the rest of the room crowded round for a warm, and your private space was invaded. Fortunately the following spring and summer were much warmer.

Aston Down was a Spitfire station, but after my being there a few months, everything was put on hold to facilitate a change of use for the station. Several weeks of inactivity followed, but the Spitfires were still serviced including the RT, on the runway.

The surrounding area of the airfield had been acquisitioned at the outbreak of war, including a productive farm and lands, which the RAF kept in good productive order. It was now late summer, and the wheat and corn harvest was due to be brought in on the farm. The wing commander of Aston Down asked for two WAAF volunteers to help with some other RAF volunteers, plus the regular farm hands to get in the harvest. We would have to be prepared to start early, and work late and be able to ride a bicycle to the farm, meals would be at the farm. Myself and another WAAF volunteered, collected our bicycles and early next morning were off to the farm. The farmhouse typically had a large kitchen and stone-flagged floor, cooking range, and a long wooden table for farmhands' mealtimes. The staff, as far as I can remember, were two old-time farmhands, two RAF lads, the gaffer, and us two extra hands.

The weather was perfect for harvesting; the sun shone and the corn was golden ripe, the grain was cut and stooked the old fashioned way, stooking is now out of fashion and would probably be too labour intensive these days. It is basically this — the grain is cut by machine, which it then tied in sheaves, these sheaves are stacked in groups of six to form a wigwam, the wigwams are formed in lines across the field, the air can then circulate through the grain, and if it should rain, the rain runs down through the stalks into the ground, thus avoiding the sheaves lying in sodden ground, where it could start sprouting again and become useless. The sun shone without fail every day, we went from the farm to the fields, on a tractor drawn trailer, and returned to the farm for meals.

After a few warm days the sheaves were dry, and ready for making into a large stack. This involved one to pitch and toss, and one to catch at the top by pitch fork, and gradually build the stack higher and higher by placing each bundle, corn to the centre, stalk facing outwards, moving round all the time. It was hard work, but rewarding to feel the stack building around you, tiring but exhilarating. As the stack got higher, a ladder was placed to rest at the side of the stack, I was never allowed at the very top, but I got halfway, then slid bottom-wise down the ladder, feet first, which I enjoyed.

The other job that wasn't so good was the winnowing with the threshing machine. The sheaves were fed into the threshing machine where it was separated from the stalk, the grain spurting out into sacks, and the chaff deposited in a pile, underneath the thresher, to be raked out and taken away. This was another of my jobs — dusty, grubby, hot, sticky, sweaty, and I was glad when that job was finished.

The harvest was finally in, and we all gathered for a harvest supper in the kitchen, around the big wooden table at the farm — it was very good too!

That was the end of an interesting experience. My skin was two shades darker, my hair two shades lighter from the sun, and I'm sure a few pounds lighter myself, but that was not quite all. I was told the wing commander requested my presence in his office, where he thanked me for my assistance with the harvest, and said all the 'hands' at the farm during those few weeks, including myself, were to have a bonus of £20, in lieu of helping out and the extra hours involved. Also, if I had any request for extra leave, he would consider it. I thought very quickly — Ken was operational still at Waterbeach. Cambridge bomber crew losses were very high, and our time was very short, so I asked if it was possible to get an exchange posting to a station near Cambridge to give us more time together — time, that elusive thing during the war years. 'Wingco' promised to see what he could do. Within a month an exchange posting came through with a WAAF stationed at Kirton Lindsey, Lincolnshire who had requested a posting to Gloucestershire for family reasons. It was all arranged, and Kirton Lindsey became my next destination for myself and my kitbag.

Kirton Lindsey had been a peacetime station and our accommodation was in ex-married quarters. Ken and I were able to meet from time to time now that we were nearer. Lincoln was a good meeting place, as the station bus did daily trips into the town. One favourite tea spot was in the services canteen at the top of the hill near the cathedral, which I remember as a homely room with nice cups and saucers and cress sandwiches. There was also the TocH; these service canteens were a haven for us, the Salvation Army, and the WI etc. Bless 'em all. Thank you! The station bus took us back to camp Kirton Lindsey and there was always a bed in the sergeants' mess for Ken. These short visits helped the wartime separations along.

I decided to surprise Ken one day. I booked in by phone for bed and breakfast for myself at an accommodation address in Waterbeach village, and took the train to Cambridge. I rang Ken in the sergeants' mess with a message to meet me in Cambridge, around teatime. We had a good evening with a visit to the cinema — I think the film was the Great Waltz, with the music of Tales from the Vienna Woods. Am I right? I think so. Then we took the service bus back to Waterbeach where Ken had to report in for eleven o'clock as air crew 'OPS'. I had a good idea where my accommodation was, as it was right in the centre of the village, which is where I got off the bus, and Ken continued on the bus to the camp.

Waterbeach village was in complete darkness — not a chink of light anywhere. I had a small torch to follow my directions, and I knocked on the door, but no one came, not even a dog barked. What could I do next? Hmmm... The whole village slumbered behind darkened windows, I decided to walk on further into the village, where perhaps there would be signs of life. Coming to the end of the street, I took a road to the right and passed a farmhouse just off the road, I could hear a cow faintly mooing. A little further on at the end of the lane I came to a red telephone box. I thought there might be a telephone book in there, but they had all been removed for military security. Now why had I not made a note of the telephone number — remember to learn that lesson! I had got used to the semi-darkness by now and realised there were only fields around, I had got myself into this situation, so I must get myself out — it was time to make a decision. There was nothing else I could do — I slept in the telephone box, crouched in the corner! The night sounds were eerie, the hoot of owls, strange animal noises — a fox, I think, but I was safe in my red turret.

The faint light of dawn came at last, I could hear sounds of movement from the farm, so I got up, dusted myself down, and emerged from my shelter. My watch said 6.30am. I made my way to the farm hoping someone could tell me the first morning train, the farmer was surprised but helpful, and I was able to catch the early morning train.

I caught the early morning train back to Cambridge, then Kirton Lindsey, and my night shift. Ken meanwhile was unaware of all this until his next letter from me. Where the mix-up occurred I shall never know. Maybe the dates were misinterpreted, which can easily be done with a telephone call.

A footnote to all this: Years later it came about there was a gentleman in Waterbeach writing about the village in wartime and its association with the RAF. There was a pub in the village, where returning bomber crew from raids over Germany would meet and gradually unwind, thankful to be alive. At the pub there are — or were — the names of returning bomber crew written on the walls. I wrote to him with my humble experience, and had a nice letter back, saying my phone box was still there, but the Post Office was intending to replace them with modern ones, but he said he would try to get my particular telephone box saved for its memories — a nice thought, but I doubt the Post Office would consider it; everything has to move with the times.

My time at Kirton Lindsey was spent partly at a fixer on the outskirts of the camp, and partly at a fixer at Hibblestow, some miles away. A 'fixer' was a RT (Radio Telephone) unit housed in a pencil-like brick building, away from other contacts. There was room for only an RT operator and one telephonist. The RT equipment was manned 24 hours a day. There was a one-bar electric fire, which came in useful for a certain amount of warmth and for making toast from slices of bread, and a lump of margarine scrounged from the breakfast table. Teabags and sugar were provided from the mess, and we collected some milk from the farm on our way at the end of the lane and field where the fixer was. There was a high wall around the fixer, with a narrow iron gate, which was kept locked once you were inside.

Ex-married quarters was an improvement on Nissen huts. We were allowed a cwt of coal per house. There was just the one fire in the downstairs room, two other girls and myself were in the upstairs room. We didn't see much of the fire, but they were quite a good crowd.

One morning I awoke with a very sore throat and my neck was swollen. I reported to the MO. he took one look and then things moved fast. He said, 'Go and get your washing gear and toothbrush, talk to no one, and report to sick bay, You have mumps.' They were afraid of it spreading round the camp. I duly reported to sick bay and was promptly put in the isolation room after the initial temperature was taken. No one was allowed to come near me, my food was left outside the door for me to collect. My neck swelled till I looked like a bullfrog. I really did feel isolated. My room was on the ground floor and overlooked a grassy area, when I was feeling better I climbed out of the low window in my room and had a walk around the grass. There was no one about — it was good! After two weeks I was allowed home on leave for ten days. Miraculously no one else on the camp went down with mumps, so the MO did the right thing. Where I caught it from, goodness knows.

My next posting was to a fixer just outside of Scunthorpe. It was civvy billets here in the town of Scunthorpe, the shifts were different to fit in with civilian routine. Ken was still operational and was on his 23rd bombing raid, when his aircraft was hit by enemy fire. They were limping home across the Channel, in their final stages and attempting to make the English coast. Ken was front-gunner and could see the sea rushing up to meet them, the plane was losing height but the pilot just made land before crashing. The captain shouted to get out quickly before the plane caught fire, Ken's arm had been broken in the crash, and he was unable to apply much leverage to extricate himself but the crew dragged him out, snow was lying on the ground, and it was bitterly cold, he was taken to Ely Hospital, where his arm was set above the elbow, but after a few days it had to be reset, and he developed pneumonia, probably from a combination of shock and lying for some time in the snow afterwards. His arm was never very good after that and set stiffly and he was 'grounded' from flying, and posted to Swinderby for airfield control and a few weeks later to what was, at first, an unknown destination overseas.

After six weeks his service address was Dum Dum RAF Station, India. He was given two days' embarkation leave at short notice. I was unable to obtain leave, leave was becoming increasingly difficult, as we now know, D-Day was approaching. After his two days' leave he had to report to Blackpool where he was in civvy billets. No one knew what was likely to happen in those days, and if we would ever see each other again. Was it possible we could meet in the next few days? were my thoughts.

My RT fixer companions were good friends, and they said they would cover my day shift, and anything else that was incurred. I rang the signals officer at Kirton Lindsey to tell him that my duties for the next two days were completely covered, and explained the reason why. The reply was, if I went, I would be on a charge.

Early the next morning I left after my night shift and hitchhiked my way to Blackpool (I do not encourage any girl these days to do this; this was wartime and totally different from today). Arriving in Blackpool the population seemed to be one sea of RAF personnel, it was going to be like looking for a needle in a haystack. I came to a bridge and weighed up the situation (you know my old adage by now). An RAF sergeant was passing and I asked him if he happened to know a Sergeant Ken Norman. He thought a while, then said 'No, but he might be able to find me some information, and to be back on the bridge in one hour's time, when he might have some news.' Needless to say I was there, and who should be there, but Ken. It was unbelievable! The sergeant had checked records, found him, and here he was. We were able to wander around and say everything we wanted to, it was fantastic luck. We had a meal together. RAF personnel on embarkation orders had to be in billets by 10pm. I stayed at a friend's house that night, whom I had known from my days in Bristol.

Ken's departure was to be about ten o'clock the next morning from the parade ground. I was able to watch the departure of the convoy from a discreet distance as it drove off. Ken thought I might be there, and was looking out of the back of a convoy lorry. We were able to exchange a farewell wave: I wasn't to see him again for another two years; India was his final destination where he was an air field controller. I hitchhiked back to Scunthorpe and nightshift. Two days where at last our world had come temporarily together.

The signals officer had visited the fixer to check on me whilst I was away, and questioned my accomplices (satisfactorily). I never heard any more about it. Under the circumstances, he must have relented.

Chapter 6

Scunthorpe seemed very tame after my adventure. There was not very much going on in the town, although there was a good services place to go, just off the main street. I think it was run by the Salvation Army — whoever, many thanks! Later in the year I was posted to a 'homer' station RT. This was identical in structure to the fixer in appearance, ie a pencil-shaped brick construction in a field away from outside contact. A homer gave a bearing, minus 180 degrees from an aircraft's transmission, and relayed it back by RT to the aircraft if the aircraft required to return to base. A fixer was in a group of three, staged at different locations from the main base, where the transmission fix was relayed back by 'land' line to the 'Ops' room. Here the fixes were plotted from three angles across a large table map and where the three fixer lines crossed, the Ops room relayed this position back by RT to the pilot as the present position of the aircraft.

One day at the homer I had a group of trainee pilots come, to see how the homing system worked. There were about eight of them, plus the officer in charge. As you can tell, Homer was very crowded, normally, holding two of us. The officer asked me to demonstrate 'homing' in co-operation with an arranged aircraft, flying I knew not where. The aircraft transmitted, I proceeded as usual without any problem. Then suddenly things went haywire. What was the problem? With all these pilots looking on, I went hot and cold inside, but thinking quickly, I said, 'Has anyone gone up the stairs? (The stairs led to the aerials and other equipment). Of course, two of them had gone investigating, and their presence in the loft interrupted the transmission signal. They apologised, and that was the end of that. I did wonder if they were trying to catch me out. Are you out there, you two lads — 1945/6? If so, I would like to have a word with you!

I was billeted in the nearest village to the homer, which was between Malvern and Worcester. The lady of the house lived on her own, and was called Nellie by everyone. There were five girls billeted there — four land girls and myself. Nellie was quite strict with all of us, she had to be, there was an American camp near Malvern, where they held occasional dances, and Nellie felt responsible for us. The girls were a grand bunch and full of fun.

Nellie had to go into hospital for a week. She put me in charge of the meals, and looking after the chickens, also to make sure the house was locked up at nights and that the electric iron was not left on, but all was well.

Dad came up to see me for the day, and I was able to show him around. Nellie made a fuss of him and all the best china and cakes came out. It was a good day. Otherwise life was uneventful.

The war ended in Europe in May 1945. It seemed to pass quietly in the village although we realised it was a great day. There was little to do at the homer, but we still had to be functional. My telephonist occasionally didn't turn up, and it was very lonely on the night shift. The small radio was great company, usually tuned in to AFN in the small hours of the morning and after we were officially told to stand down for the night. Val Munro was my favourite, with his silky tones of 'You'll never know' — great!

Sometimes, in the deep silence outside of the surrounding outer wall of the homer, I would hear strange noises, and hold my breath. Common sense would tell me it was the cattle in the field scratching their backs on the brick wall, and snorting, but could it be someone trying to climb the wall? It was a bit scary. I think my nerves were getting frayed.

There was a day when the equipment didn't function. I rang my base station, Kirton Lindsey. They told me to change a fuse and where to find the replacement, which I did. There was a loud Bang! and I felt a shock go through me. I was all right — shaken but unstirred. Being older now and wiser perhaps, I think I should have been told to switch off the power first! The equipment was back in action — mission accomplished.

The war in Europe ended with much joy in the country, quite rightly, but the services had to be demobbed gradually, so as not to flood the employment market. It was first in, first out, but for our forces in the Far East, India and Burma, it was far from over. There was a feeling that the boys being demobbed from the European zone would get all the jobs before them. This was a real possibility and it meant a lot to them. Newspapers printed on air mail paper were arriving and circulating around the stations in India. Jobs were advertised in *the Times*, which could not be applied for by the Far East forces. Each serviceman was given a number and category, depending on the time of enlisting. The word was passed around that numbers 44 in the Royal Navy were being demobbed. As an example, Ken's group was 22, so you can see why there was such a strong feeling amongst the Far East servicemen.

English newspapers printed articles and pictures of GI brides being taken on the *Queen Mary* to America, which in effect was like a red rag to a bull to the servicemen. Questions were asked: Why couldn't the *Queen Mary* pick up servicemen from India on the way back to England? It seemed, so it was said, the *Queen Mary* could not sail through the Panama Canal. I don't know if this was true but you can understand the disquiet amongst the Far East servicemen, even to the point of mutiny at one point, as the word spread from Delhi to Dubai stations. The ringleaders were, I believe, court-martialled, which I think was a bit harsh under the circumstances.

The Far East war had ended with the Hiroshima bomb, but planes were still flying from India to Chong Qing, China's capital at the time. The route taken was called the Himalayan Route, over the 'hump'. It was a dangerous scene of combat, protecting the supply planes flying between India and China. Ken sent me a lovely sapphire ring, with the most intense blue stone. It had come from Ceylon, I believe this is the only place this intense blue is found. However, our war was not over.

One day in February 1946, he had a message relayed to him from HQ to get packed in 24 hours to catch a Dakota plane to Bombay, to board a troopship for England. He needed no second bidding.

In Bombay he boarded the troopship *Circassia*. The ship had been going to Japan but had developed engine trouble, this had been dealt with in Bombay and it was decided to return to England with some of the servicemen, all ranks, from India. Because of the change of plans, there was little fresh food on board, which meant things like reconstituted potatoes, which of course the troops accepted until they heard from the kitchen personnel that the officers' mess was getting fresh potatoes. There was a concerted answer from the other ranks: Whilst there were fresh potatoes, the whole ship should get fresh potatoes until they ran out, after that, everyone would have reconstituted potatoes. The war was over, everyone was the same, and Civvy Street was going to be a very different place and world. Every man was as good as whatever he put into that world — and so it was.

On board on the way back, three men developed scarlet fever. They were landed at Port Said, and put into quarantine at a hospital there, any other servicemen who had not been inoculated was also put in quarantine and left behind.

The journey continued after this, and the *Circassia* was eventually sailing up the Firth of Clyde to Greenock, and the troops began to feel they were really home.

The demob centre fitted them up with demob suits, shoes, overcoat and six weeks' pay (I think) plus a railway warrant home.

In the meantime, things were happening in my area. Mum had a serious operation in February 1946, and needed much looking after. There was no one else at home, as Dad was still at work, he applied for compassionate discharge for me, getting statements from the doctor and the local police. My discharge was granted in March 1946; under these circumstances there were no demob suits, or other entitlements, but I felt I had done my bit and I was needed more at home. My train warrant to Bristol was for 1st April.

Ken, on landing and demob, was able to get a message to me through Kirton Lindsey sergeants' mess the day before he left, to say he would be officially demobbed on 1st April and would be catching the train to Bristol on that day. I was able to get a message back through the same grapevine, to say, 'So am I, 1st April, our rail lines will cross at Birmingham. Whoever is first there, wait on the station.' All went according to plan, with just about an hour's wait. It was quite incredible. Within an hour, we were ready to start our journey home together, and have a very long chat, as you might guess. We had a pot of tea on Temple Meads Station where we parted temporarily to go to our separate homes. Tea at Temple Meads Station, Bristol? Very mundane after all that had happened to us! *No*, it seemed like the Ritz on that occasion.

Mum was really very poorly, and I was glad to be able to do things for her. I was coming down the stairs one day and happened to look out of the landing window, which looked out onto the road behind, and there, looking around, were two WAAF SPs (Special Police). I carried on down the stairs, and told Mum to be prepared for visitors, there was no need to tell her to 'look ill' — she really did! A knock came at the front door and there were the two SPs. Was I 468342 WAAF? 'Yes I was,' I told them. 'Could they come in?' 'Yes of course.' They took only one look at Mum to see I wasn't 'swinging the lead', and we parted on good terms. It seemed a pity for them to have wasted their time but I suppose they themselves were filling in time, waiting for their demob. It was still an unreal world, which hadn't settled down. Ken was also called at his home by the medical officer because of his contact with scarlet fever on the boat. He was told to report to Horfield Barracks, if he felt ill. The tentacles of the military reach far and wide; ours was not to question why, but make sure you don't step out of line!

Like so many ex-servicemen, Ken was keen to get a job. He applied for the police force and the fire brigade. He was accepted for the fire brigade, which he was pleased about, his two months' training commenced at Newton

Abbot, the headquarters for fire brigade training. On joining the brigade he was required to state his preferences for a permanent station when he finished his course and had passed out. His choice of stations were Bristol, Taunton and Weston-super-Mare. As it turned out, he didn't get any of these. Bristol would only take married men, Taunton and Weston-super-Mare considered the shortage of housing for single men, and so he was finally posted to Barnstaple, Devon.

We had never been to Barnstaple and decided to go and have a look. We took the train to Taunton where we changed for the little cross-country train to Barnstaple which took two hours, and stopped at every little station, but on arrival at Barnstaple, and walking to the town along the riverside, we were agreeably surprised and liked the town very much. It was just our kind of town.

It was now early June. Mum was feeling much better and able to manage on her own, and Ken and I arranged to be married on 29th June 1946, which was at the end of his fire brigade course. We had the Monday and Tuesday of the following week free, before Ken started his new job the following Wednesday. At this point, a week before the wedding, we didn't have anywhere to live in Barnstaple. Ken could not get any leave to flat-hunt, so on 23rd June I took the train to Barnstaple and scoured the town for a vacant place — there was nothing. One last ray of hope — someone told me to try Mrs Binny at the Golden Fleece. I did; she said there was a possibility, but she would take me to see it first, I was willing to look at anything, she took me to some third-floor rooms, at the top of an old house in the main street. It was very cobwebby and had obviously never been used for years, it reminded me of Miss Haversham's room in *Great Expectations.*

There was one very large room with a high, ornate moulded ceiling, and a tiny little fireplace. The kitchen, as such, was quite small with an ancient electric cooker, and a bay window, partially shared with the adjoining bedroom, which was quite plain compared with the ornate ceiling of the main room, there was a trapdoor in the ceiling. The bathroom was one floor down, shared with the occupiers of the second-floor flat below, we only met them once, I expect they were not too pleased with the arrangements, but then neither were we. There was no arrangement for hot water on our floor, but there was a stone sink and cold water tap, where a window looked out onto a narrow courtyard and some small cottages. The rent was £1 a week. I had no choice but to accept.

Just before our wedding, Mrs Fry had asked to see Ken and myself. We met her in the drawing room of her house, she was very interested in our service life and our fire service posting to Barnstaple. As we left she gave us a sealed envelope, wishing us happiness and saying, 'Tell Mann (Granfer) to pick all the roses you would like for your wedding bouquet from my garden,' which he did. They were lovely. The envelope contained a cheque for £20.

On the following Thursday, 27th June, I arranged for our small amount of furniture and china to be transported to Barnstaple. Including, two armchairs — not new, but recovered in leather. Furniture was on dockets, and utility table and chairs, bedstead and tallboy, the first of that kind to be made after the war — practical, affordable and surprisingly well made, and probably collectors' items now. It was transported in a small furniture van to Barnstaple, including myself. After seeing it all safely installed, I would have liked to have made the removers a cup of tea, they had been very good at humping it all up three flights of stairs, but at the time there was no electricity. After they left, I set about removing the cobwebs and old net curtains — they were grey with age! It was looking better already. The train took me back to Bristol, I was exhausted but 'best foot forward' — it was our wedding day in 48 hours, Ken would be home the next day from Newton Abbot, and we had somewhere to live.

It was a lovely day on Saturday 29th June, and everything went well. The guests came back to Rose Cottage for a meal, which Mum and Dad had managed to get together with the help of my aunts from London and Southend. Ken's mum, sisters, gran, grandad, aunts and uncles came. It was quite a gathering.

At about 4.30, Ken and I left to catch the train for Barnstaple together with a collection of wedding gifts we had been given on the day. Believe it or not, one was a meatsafe with some saucepans inside. I don't expect many of you will know what a meatsafe is or looks like — well, before refrigerators were available to most people, the meatsafe was hung in the coolest place, quite often on a shaded outside wall. The sides were perforated with holes, to allow a current of air to flow through, hopefully keeping the meat fresh — just think how lucky you are today!

The train for the first part of the journey to Taunton was full. Regardless of the fact that we had first class tickets to mark the occasion, we had to stand in the corridor. On the train to Barnstaple there was a seat, but no corridor or first class. There was something calming about this little train, though, that trundled along stopping at every station along the way.

At last we arrived at our new home. It was quite late and we didn't know yet of any restaurant of worth, so we settled for fish and chips from a shop that sold locally caught fish, it was at the bottom of the high street where our flat was. It served our purpose well, and was good.

The next day was spent cleaning up the rooms, and slapping some green paint on the landing to brighten it up with some paint that Dad had as surplus to requirements that had come in the van, we also explored the town for some food shopping the next day. Basic food acquired, on the Monday afternoon we cycled to Croyde Bay and its sandy beach.

Ken was due to start at the fire station on the Wednesday. His shift work was 24 hours on and 24 hours off. Food was still very short in the country and on ration. There was an extra allowance for fire service, heavy-duty jobs, and manual work, which gave them the entitlement of an extra bread ration. The theme running through every day was, 'What can we have for dinner today!' There was always a good supply of fresh fish in Barnstaple, caught locally, the butcher's sausages were quite good, and a favourite of ours was vegetable casserole. Porridge and kippers were my main sustenance when Ken was on his 24 hour shift in the fire brigade. It seems very austere by today's standards of fancy cooking but we survived and everyone was in the same position. One day the butcher said in a hushed voice, 'I have some sweetbreads today — would you like some?' I had never sampled sweetbreads or seen them before, but not wishing to show my ignorance, I said, 'Yes please,' but we didn't really like them.

Coal was rationed to a cwt a week and delivered into a hole in the wall on the third floor landing. I always hated passing that hole in the dark. We had a coal fire in the little fireplace every other day when Ken was off duty, every alternate day it was the one-bar electric fire in the kitchen. The winter of 1946/47 was very, very cold, the snow around Barnstaple was banked up against the sides of the road until April. Electricity was a shilling in the slot to a meter at the bottom of the stairs, by the front door; it was high up on the wall, and I kept a box to stand on in the hall, so that I could reach it I always made sure the meter was 'fed' before it got dark if Ken was on duty; the stairs were dark and creepy and the shilling in the slot didn't last very long, but it was a different place in the daytime — we managed!

I think the kitchen and bedroom must have been one big room at one time; this would account for the bay window being partly in both rooms with a 'step over' connecting the two rooms. The window itself provided a view of the end of the High Street, to the bridge beyond and just around the corner was the fire station. From the window, there was a good view of the fire engine turning out with bells clanging when the alarm goes off.

With some of the money we had put by, I bought a brand new Singer sewing machine, one of the first off the production line after the war. We had to wait two months for its delivery. The day we collected it, the snow was lying thick on the ground and the pavements were so slippery that we had to slide the machine back to the flat on its case, like a sledge. It was a very worthwhile purchase and kept us supplied with clothes for 50 years and more. My daughter has it now and together we made an evening dress for my granddaughter's first 'occasion' — the end of term dance. The other big item of the day was a cream stainless steel kitchen cabinet, quite unusual for the times, but that has followed us around in different houses also.

The house was very old and the timbers creaked at night, Ken had put bolts on the doors, but the bedroom ceiling trap door scared me sometimes. I felt there was someone up there and I held my breath the better to listen, and then try and convince myself it was only mice.

But there were other things to occupy my mind, for which we had acquired a Silver Cross green and cream pram and a blue carry cot. We looked forward to that occasion.

Chapter 7

Our brand new baby arrived on 20th June 1947. He was beautiful.

A fortnight before the expected arrival, Ken was informed he was to be transferred to Weston-super-Mare fire station in two weeks' time — it was a bit of a bombshell to us. Nothing could alter the decision, the only consideration was he could stay until after the baby was born, and then take his two weeks holiday due leave, then report to Weston-super-Mare station.

Roger and I came home seven days after he was born, which left very little time before Ken had to leave for Weston. He didn't have any accommodation in the new town, but he was allowed to sleep at the station. Very occasionally he was able to come home for weekends, by hitchhiking on the Saturday, and returning by train on the Sunday. The hitchhiking was difficult on the Barnstaple to Taunton road because of the lack of traffic. Life was quite grim!

Roger was progressing well, thank goodness. I had two days with a fever, when I couldn't go out at all. There wasn't anyone we knew in the town, but like everything else, you just get on with it. One weekend when Ken was home we took Roger to Rock Park Barnstaple, where there was a baby show, and he won first prize, so you see we were getting some things right!

One day I looked out into the courtyard below from the landing room window, where I had been putting Roger outside to sleep for the fresh air. The pram was always left in the hall, as it was difficult to manage up and down the stairs and I carried him down. From the landing room window I was horrified to see a stooped, unkempt man with long hair and beard. I had briefly spoken to an elderly woman who lived in the cottages but this was different. Ken made some enquiries when he next came home, and it appeared the man was really quite a young man who lived with his mother in the cottages, he was very eccentric and spent his time dealing in stocks and shares, quite successfully I expect, and was often seen roaming the town. Even so, I could never put Roger there again. We went for a walk every day instead, rain or shine, through the town and down by the river, to the very pleasant park.

Being newcomers to the town we had very few acquaintances, there was one, Jen, the wife of a fireman who came to Barnstaple about the same time as us, who I met occasionally, but time hung heavily.

There was no possibility of accommodation in Weston, although Ken had tried everything, there was nothing available after the war. One day I packed a small bag with things for Roger, plus sandwiches, put Roger in his carry cot and caught the train to Weston-super-Mare, intending to catch the bus from there to Bristol and Frenchay but I wanted to see Ken first, to let him know where I was. It was not yet time for him to come off duty, so we sat on a seat opposite the fire station, which was just across the road from the seafront, Ken happened to look out of the control room window and was amazed to see this group of familiar faces across the road.

He was given permission to come over and see us, and when his shift ended we all caught the bus to Frenchay. Mum and Dad had a big surprise too! Mum quickly made Roger a bed out of a drawer from the blanket box, Ken went back the next day for his night shift, and Roger and I stayed at home for the week. Then it was back to Barnstaple, but the break had done us good. All channels had been tried by Ken to find us accommodation, but it was impossible, and on his next weekend at home, he had a proposition to talk over.

Situated in a village called Banwell, about five miles from Weston, he had heard there was a collection of Army huts that were now lying empty. Ex-servicemen, with families but without accommodation, were taking some of them over, unofficially, as 'living quarters', because of the housing shortage three other firemen in the same position — one Royal Navy, one Army, one Bomber Command RAF, and one young lad who had been a Bevan Boy, were interested. The huts were just as they had been left — one large long hut, plus the corporal's room at the entrance, with the usual small round stove in the middle. There was no running water, that had to be fetched by bucket from a tap about 50 yards away. There were no connecting drains, so it would have to be an Elsan in the corporal's room — not a rosy picture to have to paint. What did I think? I did not hesitate. I knew exactly what to expect. My thoughts were, at least we should all be together, and I was willing to make a go of it. So it was, we were on the move again, literally to be 'squatters' but 'ex-service squatters', and all in the same boat.

To anyone who may read this — you may think, 'How could they?' But, when there is no alternative you have no options and have to get on with it. I just want to record how tough things were after the war, for the ones who came out of it, just wanting to live the best way we could survive. Ex

-service folk had a camaraderie that was lacking in Civvy Street. We had little money, and you couldn't save on service pay, but we were alive and thankful.

Mum and Dad wanted to mortgage their house to help us get started somewhere, but we couldn't let them do that, even if it had been available — but it was good to know I had parents who cared. First impressions of the site were quite good. The huts occupied two fields, with the huts arranged around the perimeter, and a large area of grass in the centre. The area in the vicinity was countryside, and there was a bus service to Weston at the top of the lane leading down from the main road. Most of the huts were occupied, but there was one at the bottom of the field, which had a fair piece of land around it, mentally we thought we could cultivate it. On entering, the hut seemed a vast open space, and our little bit of furniture seemed swallowed up in it, but we soon added a few things. We had brought our state-of-the-art kitchen cabinet, which took pride of place beside the wooden kitchen table covered with a colourful tablecloth. For cooking I had a two-funnel, paraffin burner stove, which could accommodate a small metal oven on the top, the paraffin burner also served to boil a kettle or a metal bucket for washing.

Ken eventually managed to get an old kitchen range and install it, instead of the small Army stove. This was a great help in the winter for larger quantities of water and heating in general, but for the moment we managed with the paraffin stove and a 'stand-up' bath in Roger's baby bath — where there's a will there's a way!

No one in the compound paid any rent in the beginning, the Council recognised we were not going away, and accepted us as genuine with the need of a roof over our head, however simple. Eventually every hut was charged eight shillings a week rent, and electric meters were installed in the entrance of each hut, and we were able to run a one-bar electric fire if required. I had to do something about curtains for the windows; the only material available was quite flimsy dress material, 36in wide and on dockets, but it had to do, and I quickly ran them up on my machine. At 36in and after allowing for very small hems, they scarcely met when I drew them across.

One plus sign was Roger was able to get plenty of fresh air and progressed, every day he was sleeping outside in his pram. There was a grocery shop in Banwell two miles away, which I walked to with the pram twice a week, taking a lane that avoided the main road but ran parallel with it. The butcher called once a week with his van although there was very little he could offer. The baker also called at Summers Lane.

Yes, Summers Lane was our postal address. We had also acquired a puppy called Paddy, a highly intelligent cross breed, from my thoroughbred spaniel at Frenchay, called 'Whimpy' after the aircraft Ken was air crew in during the war years,

Fetching the water in two buckets from the tap 50 yards away became part of our routine, and disposal was a very large hole in the plot of land that was now our garden. Ken cycled to work at the fire station. In his off-duty time, he was attempting to make a partition to divide our very long room, but wood was scarce and was on permits only. Cycling home one day, he passed a business that was selling off strips of 'off cuts' from materials they were using for the making of 'prefabs', which were temporary bungalow homes to help ease the housing shortage. The firm was on the outskirts of Weston. These housing prefabs, although a temporary measure, had all the modern conveniences inside, and were really a very good substitute — if you could get one. As it wasn't to be for us, Ken purchased a whole lot of these strips, they were about 9" wide, and he attached them to one of the horizontal rafters, where they hung like streamers, until they were anchored by a strip across the bottom. It was an improvement, at least we had a division between the end of the hut to the bedroom.

The oven over the paraffin burners worked quite well, except that you had to be careful to keep the wicks clean, and not to turn the wick up too high, when it would smoke disastrously; it would cook our small ration of meat quite well, but was not controllable enough for a casserole. We had some very good neighbours, the Tilleys, with a son and daughter, Nancy. A young lad of Roger's age, David Westlake, Nancy and Roger were the best of friends, the two boys had small three-wheeled tricycles which they raced along the tarmac path that bordered the huts, they didn't turn the pedals, but just scooted along with their feet; good exercise and plenty of fresh air, one of the plus points of Summers Lane.

One Christmas morning Jane Tilley asked us round to sample her home-made blackberry wine, later in the day. The Christmas Eve, Christmas Day and Boxing Day shifts were shared out equally at the fire station, to give everyone in the brigade a chance to spend part of Christmas at home. Ken's shift was for Christmas day and Boxing Day night, that year. We had a chicken for Christmas dinner, which I would cook for the evening of 25th, when Ken came home. I arranged to call round to the Tilleys with Roger, later in the afternoon, and put the chicken in the oven on low. The wine was excellent, and the company, but when Roger and I returned home we found the paraffin stove under the oven had been smoking and the chicken was shades of black and grey with soot, although it did appear to be cooked. We had only been away 30 minutes (close your ears all you firemen). My precious chicken was hardly recognisable. The burner must have smoked like a chimney. I was horrified — what do you do under those circumstances? I thought I'd try washing it with water. Have you ever tried mixing soot with water? Don't! It was a complete mess. All was not quite lost. I carefully skinned the chicken completely, it was cooked inside, and I cut suitable slices off to keep warm over the vegetables, which were now cooking. All was well; the dinner was enjoyed. I didn't mention it till a long time afterwards — there's no point in spoiling someone else's Christmas, is there? What the eye doesn't see the heart won't grieve over!

The seasons rolled around. Roger was now interested in everything that moved, unscrewed or went 'brum brum'. The group of three — Nancy, David and Roger — were as happy as larks, and free as the birds. In late summer we picked blackberries from the many hedgerows in the locality. A man with a trailer came round once a week in September; he would buy the blackberries by the bucketful, which were tipped into two wooden barrels on the trailer. These were used in the dyeing trade at the time. Paddy was a happy member of the family and enjoyed everything that was going on. With Roger moving about as fast as a streak of lightening Ken had to make a door for the second partition, as the end of the hut had become the coalhouse and for some unexplainable reason it held a fascination for Roger, we found him trying to eat a piece of coal one day. He was a great lover of Dinky toys, which were very popular with all little boys then. Of course, he had a Dinky fire engine — the small rubber tyres were always coming off and getting lost, but replacements were available.

In 1949, on a cold morning in February, our lovely daughter Susan was born. Ken was on night duty, but Jane Tilley said I could call on her if needed. It was six o'clock in the morning. I felt quite well, but thought I should call the midwife who was to attend me. It was a frosty morning with a light sprinkling of snow covering the ground, and the compound was slumbering, I had no wish to disturb them at that hour. The telephone box was a little way away, crossing the main road at the top of Summers Lane, and a short way down another lane; there was no other way of communication. Roger was sleeping soundly in his new cot; Ken had made it with dowelling sides that locked when pulled up, to stop him from climbing out, or falling out; he was now getting very venturesome. I considered it safe to leave him under the circumstances. I made it to the telephone box without mishap, and called the midwife, who said she would be there in half an hour. I called Ken at the fire station, he had previously got permission to come straight away if necessary. I was quite relieved to be going back down Summers Lane and in sight of home. Everything was still quiet around, and Roger was still sleeping when I got home. I put on plenty of water to boil on the stove, and the kettle ready for a cup of tea. Ken and the Midwife arrived about the same time, and Sue, half an hour later — 28th February 1949. She was lovely. Ken was able to take some leave off to help out in the first week, and I was soon up and about again.

With the arrival of Sue, we applied again to have our name down on the housing list in Weston-super-Mare where they had a points system for any new houses that became available. We were seriously thinking of trying for a transfer to Bristol fire brigade. Weston housing authority replied that we were living outside of their boundary at Banwell, and couldn't be considered and to apply to Congresbury, which was our housing area. The reply from Congresbury was that they couldn't do anything for us, as we hadn't been living in the area before the war, and we must go back to the area, Bristol, where we had lived before the war.

We wrote to the Bristol housing authority to see what the position was, because a couple of years before the war ended, there was a notice in the local newspaper that said that any servicemen or women resident in Bristol in peacetime, pre-war, could register with the Bristol council now for housing, as it became available after the war.

Ken had been in India at the time, so with his agreement I had put his name and home address forward. Our request to Bristol council was to know the position now, six years on, with the war over four years ago. The reply we received back stunned us: 'Your house has already been allocated to a "Norman" family some time ago.' There was no other explanation, and nothing we could do. Our only hope seemed to be with Weston — at least Ken worked there. So we kept on applying and applying, although the situation seemed hopeless, but after three-and-a-half years at Summers Lane we were allocated a house in Weston.

It was unbelievable, but when we actually collected the keys and looked around the house, we were delighted. The house was at the end of a road, with quite a large garden space to cultivate, a small stream or rhyne ran along beside it. We worked hard, and with pleasure — the garden plot in a few years won Weston's 'Best Garden' prize for two consecutive years. Ken also got an allotment quite near to produce plenty of vegetables.

Roger started school when he was five in the September term at Milton Road and at seven moved to the junior school at Worle on the outskirts of Weston. In the same year Sue started school. Both schools were excellent. At Worle school Mr Bull was the headmaster, and encouraged Sue with her painting and drawing to paint a frieze of what she could see from the schoolroom window, it was then hung on the wall. Mr Jones, the second-in-command, had the reputation for demanding attention, to any boy with his mind elsewhere, a piece of chalk would come his way. He also kept an old slipper for any boy misbehaving. It was, bend over, and a few slaps with the slipper! None of this hurt, except perhaps their dignity. It probably wouldn't be considered correct today, more's the pity, but it did bring the class to life, and was a lesson well learned.

Roger and Sue had a very good grounding at Worle juniors in the early school years, which is very important. Roger from there went to Worle secondary school and took the 13+ for an entry to Bridgwater Technical, which was his choice in life. Sue, at 11+, gained a place at Weston-super-Mare grammar school.

We walked or cycled into Weston often; our favourite place was along by the old pier, and spent many a picnic there. Paddy loved the water, and would make a dash for the tide line, and then roll in the sand afterwards; he looked like a hedgehog. He enjoyed being with us, but sadly he became poorly and had to have an operation. He instinctively sensed the second appointment — the surgical smell, white coats and having to go back to the vet's house and surgery. It was not successful, so, as no more could be done for him, I had the vet come to our house, where, in his favourite place, and me holding his paw, the vet quietly put him to sleep. I said I would never have another dog — I get too attached to them. I love dogs very much, they become such friends.

As with most service establishments, promotion usually required moving house and family; this came to us in 1960 when Ken was promoted to headquarters in Taunton. This was a good move for Ken, and an opportune decision for the family. After the summer school holidays, both Sue and Roger would be starting new schools in any case, so there would be no disruption in their education. Taunton was to be our town, a county town that held something for each of us. Roger would travel by train daily to Bridgwater, and Sue would start at Bishop Fox's grammar school in the September. Ken's work, apart from his daily office routine, was travelling three nights a week to the far corners of the county for inspection and training duties at the outlying 'part time' stations. I was taking PE, games and swimming at a mixed-age junior school, plus helping a younger group to make headway happily at school. I love children of all ages, there is a trusting innocence in them that you must meet and join with them, at their level, they, in their turn, will respond. Grown-ups can be hard and crusty, maybe what their childhood and growing up has made them. I do think loving parents and good basic food provides the foundation for becoming a well balanced 'grown up'. Sermon over!

We had a cycling holiday — Ken, Roger, Sue and I — in the August school holidays in our second year at Taunton, staying at youth hostels around Devon and Cornwall. I have always loved youth hostelling. You meet like-minded individuals and groups, many from other countries, all travelling under their own steam. It is a little different now because folk can travel to the YHA in their own cars, and then go walking or cycling from that centre; it's not quite the same, but it does encourage young and old to enjoy the countryside.

Roger and Sue made new friends, the area was good for cycling, and we were able to cycle into Taunton by a route that avoided the main road. Our house was a fire brigade house. The front of the house was open plan, and the back was a fair size, which we kept in flowers and lawn with a greenhouse at the bottom, where I grew masses of tomatoes. Ken had an allotment for producing all our vegetables. Roger progressed to Taunton technical college for a two-year course.

One day a little girl from the school asked me if I would like a puppy, as they had one of a litter they wanted to find a home for. I said I couldn't really, but thanked her for asking me. She brought the puppy to school the next day, and I could not refuse! As I rode my bicycle to school, I had to find a way to get him home, and so it was he travelled in my shopping bag, hung on the handlebars, with the zip pulled along, so that he could not jump out, and his little head just peeping out over the top of the bag. He didn't seem to mind this new experience and in spite of the traffic sometimes whizzing by, we arrived home safely. I made a little bed for him in the hall and he curled up and went to sleep quite happily.

Sue and Roger were expected home from school quite soon — I wanted to surprise them. I closed the door to the hall. Sue usually arrived first and both had a little something to eat to keep them satisfied until the cooked meal with Dad came later on, their favourite was a big sugared bath bun, buttered and cut in half which I bought at a special bakers shop in the High Street on my way home. In the meantime the puppy had woken up on hearing the sound of voices coming from the kitchen, and was exploring his new surroundings and making whimpering noises, which Sue heard and she opened the door. They were amazed at what they saw. 'Where did he come from? Could we keep him? Please, please?' There was lots of smoothing and cuddling for him, which of course he thought was great. We called him Shandy because he was black with a white ruff of fur around his neck. He became a good friend of the family.

Roger had glandular fever just before his final exams at Taunton Technical College with a high temperature. The doctor, knowing his exams were crucial, gave him a good dose of penicillin, which, although he was not 100 percent, enabled him to take the exam and ensure an OND engineering pass and a four-year sandwich course, with English Electric, each year six months at Stafford University and six months practical at English Electric He graduated at the end of that time with a BSc engineering. Sue had another year to do before A levels, which she completed at Exmouth grammar school with a preliminary course at Newton Abbott College of Art and Design, leading to a three-year course at Bristol West of England College, graduating with a DipAD in art and design. They both did well.

Ken had a promotional move to Devon brigade headquarters near Exeter in June. To avoid any disruption to Roger and Sue's final years at Taunton, he travelled from Devon to Taunton until the end of the summer term.

It was to be all change — our paths were mapped out. We were on the move again.

Chapter 8

Leaving Taunton was quite sad; Roger would be leaving home for his sandwich course with English Electric in Staffordshire, just as we were leaving Taunton with all its memories — but these things have to be. Sue stayed with her friend on that final weekend at Taunton, Roger had his part-time 'pocket money' job to complete for a further month, so it was Ken, Shandy and me, with the furniture van that left the empty house. That memory is crystal-clear in my mind.

Fortunately the fire service house at Woodbury, Devon was very nice, but for us dedicated gardeners the garden was very small. Woodbury is a typical Devon village, with plenty of community spirit and travel connections to Exmouth, Exeter and Woodbury Common. Roger came home for a week before commencing his course, to check up where we now lived, and which was his bedroom. We decided he needed feeding up a bit. There was an Aga-type cooker in the kitchen, which I had always wanted; it was lovely to have an oven at the ready anytime to pop in another batch of scones.

About nine months later, we saw an advertisement in the local paper for a house to rent in West Hill, a small village near Ottery St Mary. We liked that area and went to have a preliminary look. The garden was large and overgrown, but we thought it had great possibilities; the house had leaded window panes, a front door porch, pleasing to the eye roof tiles, and a very tall chimney adjoining the slanting portion of the roof, with a small ledge halfway down for the witches to rest on — so folklore decrees! A peep through the window into the empty room made us quite sure we were going to apply for this house.

Mr Peckett, the owner, lived at Westhayes, the big house at the end of the drive, which ran by the side of the cottage. Our new home was called Westhayes Cottage. It had been a former gardener's house for Westhayes itself in 1920. Mr Peckett arranged to show us round, after which we were definitely interested, and applied in writing. We had a reply by telephone to say we could be the new tenants of Westhayes Cottage. It was the large garden that appealed to us, but I would miss my Aga-type cooker — still, you can't have everything.

The village of West Hill was about two miles from Ottery St Mary — a small town, but you could get almost everything there — approximately six to seven miles from Sidmouth, Exmouth and Budleigh Salterton. West Hill itself had, when we first went there, a small shop with the main grocery items, and the Post Office was at the bottom of the hill. The Potters owned the store. It was enlarged substantially some years later to contain the Post Office, bakery, butchers and hairdressers. Woodbury Common's expanse of heath land and heather was just two miles away, with many footpaths and walks. Shandy was delighted.

On Sue's first Christmas at West Hill, she did the job of Christmas relief postwoman. Things got very busy and Jack and the postman said they needed extra help. Sue said, 'My mum will do it,' so, much to my surprise, I became a temporary postwoman. It was good fun and pleasurable delivering the parcels and cards and the occasional brace of pheasants, all done by bicycle. That was the end of it, I thought, but one morning at six o'clock there was the sound of small stones at the bedroom window. On looking out, the other regular postman's wife was standing there, trying to attract my attention. Her husband had hurt his back — could I go down to the Post Office and help out? I agreed to be there in half an hour. Thus followed another couple of months delivering the mail by bicycle. This was at the beginning of January, calmer than the Christmas rush, and the weather unpredictable, but it was good for the complexion. I had the round covering the centre of the village. Jack was in charge, the mail was delivered in sacks in the Post Office side room, where we sorted it in order of the round. Dogs have a thing about postmen, I think. They must think we are brandishing the letters at them. I had two encounters as such: One terrier nipped my heel as I turned to go, and Jack asked them to keep their dog in till 8.30 in future. Secondly, an Alsatian rushed out and pinned me against the wall with his paws, luckily the owner came out and said 'He was only playing', but that was a bit hair-raising! In the icy weather and a layer of snow on the ground it was best to walk with a loaded bicycle. Some wooden latched gates were frozen at the latch so I climbed over the top of the gate — all part of life's rich tapestry of memories.

In the September Sue started at Newton Abbot College of Art and Design, coming home at weekends, which we looked forward to — it eased us into the time to come when she enrolled at Bristol College of Art, and would 'fly away'. At the commencement of term there, we settled her into a rented flat, as there was no student accommodation available. When we left we were sad to leave her alone, but she soon made friends at college, passing out with a Dip AD.

Back at Frenchay, Gran had died. Granfer Mann and Aunt Edie came to live with Mum and Dad, at Rose Cottage. Granfer died a year later; Aunt Edie was now practically blind as well as deaf, but she continued to live comfortably with Mum at home and was well looked after. Braille library books were a great help to her, and were delivered by post, another help was the monthly social meetings at Kingswood, arranged by the Society for the Blind. Aunt Edie had her own room on the ground floor, and joined Mum and Dad for meals.

Rose Cottage was renamed Cambray after Cambrai in France, where Dad was wounded during the First World War.

I became interested in competitions, where the task was to complete a sentence — 'I like… because…' in so many words. There were quite a lot of this type at the time on food labels, whose contents were in regular use, or worth a try to taste. My first win was a washing machine, the entry form being on a soap powder box — nothing was bought unnecessarily. This spurred me on to try more. It was a good way to pass the evenings when Ken was out on training duties. Over the following years these competitions brought us holidays to Jamaica, Tobago, Paris and Holland plus several to Majorca, but never a car; the nearest thing I got to four wheels was a pair of roller skates. I enjoyed the challenge of condensing the sentence in the shortest number of words. This type of competition is not often available now, it's just first drawn out of the hat, which is fairer, but not as much fun — no challenge.

At one of their weekends visiting us, Sue and Jim announced they were getting married. They were still at college together, and had been friends right from the beginning. Their three-year course had nearly finished, and on completion, Jim got a job in London. We were very pleased for them and the wedding was in Bristol with family and a few friends; the reception in Park Street.

Life at Westhayes Cottage continued quietly. We had a staff car, but the mileage allowance (200 miles a year) was limiting, and Ken was on call five to six nights a week. But we did lots of walking on Woodbury Common and from Woodbury Common across to Budleigh Salterton and picnics on the beach, with a local caught crab sandwich as back-up.

A few years previously I was visiting home (Frenchay) for a couple of days where Sue came out to join me. She was doing an 'end of course' thesis on the past history of Frenchay, Hambrook and Winterbourne.

When it was time for both of us to return home — Sue to Bristol, and my connection home to Devon — I went to say goodbye to Aunt Edie in her room. I always liked to give her a kiss, and squeeze her hand gently. It was then she surprised me by saying, 'Your mum is not my sister.' I didn't quite know what to say — Dad was calling from the other room to hurry as it was time for the bus. To Aunt Edie I could just communicate on my fingers. 'Who? Father?' The word I heard in reply is not for me to print at the moment. I put it at the back of my mind; the moment had gone as we rushed to catch the bus.

I never saw Aunt Edie again, as she died a few months later. How I have regretted those last moments were not longer. Aunt Edie, in her young days, although deaf, could lip-read quite well. Mum and her sisters helped her to form the written word into correct speech by forming their lips and mouth into the correct sound for the written word. New words could be difficult for her; for example, Roger for her would be spoken as 'Rogger'. So in her words, our Roger was always Rogger and Sue 'Sooee' but we never tried to change that.

As I write this now, I realise something — Aunt Edie would have been 12-13 years old when Mum was a baby, and would have understood a lot of what was being said at the time. At 12 years or thereabouts, Aunt Edie was admitted to the deaf/blind school in Bristol. This was unusual, I believe, as the school only took children up to the age of 10 years — was someone pulling the strings? Whatever the reason it was of great benefit to her, helping her with her speech and also teaching her to read a form of Braille writing, which was very useful to her in later life.

Jim had settled into his job in London and he and Sue had a flat there, Roger stayed with them for some time after he had finished his course with English Electric. Sue had a job in the Art Department at Kingston Polytechnic. Just before Christmas time, Jim was not very well, and had been to see their family doctor. One day Sheila rang to ask us if we could meet Jock and herself. We suggested my home at Frenchay, as it was about a midway point for both of us. We met, just the four of us, in the end room at home where Mum had lit the fire for us. The information that Sheila had to tell us was difficult for her to convey — Jim had leukaemia. We were sad and so sorry for Jock and Sheila — Jim was their only child. Sue, we were unaware, had known, from tests taken a short while before. Jim tried to continue his work but the treatment made him very poorly and he had to give up. Sue continued at Kingston Polytechnic as it was their only source of income, but they managed and we all hoped his treatment would be successful. They never ever complained, or gave up hope.

In 1973 Mum and Dad came to live with us at Westhayes Cottage, their large garden and their house had got too much for them. They had our two end rooms — one up, one down — and brought some of their own familiar pieces of furniture and personal things, to help them settle in. When you have lived in a house and garden for 52 years, it is difficult to leave — Frenchay had been the whole of Mum's life, and a good part of Dad's, but we did our best to make them comfortable, and they were well cared for; I think Dad was happy here — it was his disposition and his relief to know they were cared for. But Mum's memories were in Frenchay, which is only natural. They lived with us for two years, until they died within three months of each other.

Ken's retirement was coming up in 1976. We bought a second-hand Dormobile, and made plans for travelling. She was a reliable, comfortable old lady; we called her Bessie. We had a surprise party arranged for Ken at the Blue Ball, Sidford with Roger and Pam, and Sue and Jim turning up when Ken thought it was just him and I. He was greatly surprised and pleased. Jim was very poorly, but desperately wanted to come, and he managed very bravely.

We continued our walks and weekends away with the camping club, Devon section. Sue and Roger were now away from home, and Shandy had died just before Ken retired, so we were now footloose and fancy-free. We saw an article in the camping club magazine for strawberry pickers, for Wilkins, the jam makers; there was a camping field available. At the time we decided we didn't want any job to tie us down but were quite willing to do part-time jobs. This seemed like a good idea — and it was great! Strawberry picking is a hands and knees job, edging your way along the rows and rows of strawberries, resting occasionally to sample a particularly luscious, sun-warmed strawberry. At the top of the field was the Wilkins tractor and trailer where you were given a bucket and appointed a strawberry row. When your bucket was full it was taken to the trailer, weighed, and you were paid so much a bucket. You could do as many hours as you wished, the fields were open at six in the morning until around six in the evening. We usually picked in the morning and returned to Bessie for a late lunch. There were special rows of strawberries called and sold as 'Little Scarlet' — very small and sweet; a bucket of these would take three times as long to pick, but you were paid accordingly. Every year the first 'Little Scarlets' picked and jammed were sent to the Queen in a dozen jars. We made £76.64 between us over four mornings, not a princely sum but enjoyed — remember this was 1976.

On our way home we called on Sue in her flat, and stayed for a few days — of course bringing strawberries and jars of strawberry jam. It was a good time. Sue came home during her holiday time and we had many lovely walks at Budleigh and along the banks of the River Otter with Polly, her dog.

Bessie had been kitted out with matching curtains, cushion covers and crockery, the open road beckoned and we were ready to meander. We decided our first overseas adventure with her would be France. Our first point of departure was to be Plymouth and a ferry crossing to Roscoff, and a crossing to St Malo. From there on we stopped at small campsites wherever the fancy took us, moving on the next day or staying a couple of nights, phoning Sue and Rog on the way so that they knew where we were; it was not always easy to get through on the phone. We reached the south coast of France, and meandered along the coastline before turning northwards for a leisurely journey homewards. We camped at Fougeres that evening.

I tried several times to get through to Sue without success and then I rang Roger. After a long pause, he said, 'Sue is here with us and Polly, her dog. Jim has died.' It was an awful shock. For a moment I could not take it in or accept it. Roger had asked the French police to try and locate us but without success. We said we would be home as fast as we could. It took us two days to reach St Malo and catch the first ferry to England. Jock and Sheila were at home at Westhayes Cottage with Sue; they were a comfort to each other. The funeral had taken place days before when they were unable to contact us. The following day they all went to Cornwall for a few days where they had had some happy times and memories. We were so sad for Sue and for Jim and his brave fight for life.

Sue kept her flat on at Surbiton and her job at Kingston Polytechnic. It was the best thing for her to do. Words cannot say what we felt.

Chapter 9

1977

What we had seen about the Camping Club appealed to us, especially the tent camping; it took us back in memory to our cycle camping days before the war. We bought two new bicycles, Falcon Black Diamonds with 21 gears, and did quite a lot of local cycling, rejoining the YHA (Youth Hostelling Association) and the CTC (Cyclist Touring Club).

Our first weekend away was to Crowcombe Youth Hostel near Taunton. The blood was rising, the excitement was there. Yes! We would buy a lightweight tent. We did — a Robert Saunders, with two bell ends, one for keeping the spare gear packed away, when once we were in situ, the other to keep the entrance dry in wet weather, and to set up the Trangia under cover, for making an early morning mug of tea, and watching the rest of the camp come to life. A Trangia is the modern equivalent of the Primus stove, and is run on methylated spirits (widely available in France). To carry all the equipment, we had a pair of Karrimor green pannier bags for the back cycle carrier, topped with two 'Stuff Sacks', which fit on top of the panniers. A green Karrimor front bag fitted on to the handlebars, which carried all travelling details, cash, and anything important. This was detachable, with a shoulder carrying strap, this bag went everywhere with us, and was never left unattended on the bicycle. We called our tent Horace.

Many trips were made in France cycle camping, and in this country youth hostelling with the bicycles — Yorkshire Moors and Dales, the Derbyshire Dales, Wiltshire, Somerset, Gloucestershire, Surrey and Oxfordshire. In Surrey, we had our bicycles stolen, even though they were safely locked up and in view of the cafe where we had stopped for a coffee. That is a dreadful experience, to come back and find your cycle gone, not even a cut chain left, the cycles must have been lifted onto a van. They were partly insured, but the memories of their travels were part of them. Fortunately, on that day, our camping gear was not with us, as we were visiting Sue in Surbiton. Nevertheless we bought two new cycles — Claud Butlers — to continue our travels.

We decided to try a tour of Brittany. So with our 'house' on our bicycles, we set forth. This was to be our first trip with Horace abroad. What did the future hold? We set off from Westhayes Cottage early one morning, to cycle to Plymouth, and the ferry. It drizzled with rain most of the way; we stopped and ate our sandwiches under a railway bridge out of the rain, undeterred. We spent the night at YHA, Plymouth, and caught the first morning ferry to Roscoff. Boarding a ferry as a cyclist is quite an experience and good fun. As a cyclist you are entitled, and requested, to go to the front of the queue of motorists and caravans etc, this is to give the cyclist a good head start when the 'ship boarding' is signalled, and begins, then off you go as fast as you can, into the jaws and the hold of the ferry. Your bicycle must be securely attached to the rails that line the side of the hold, and the cars and caravans are lined up beside you. After detaching your front bag to take with you, you are free to go on deck. Cyclists are first on and first off, giving them time to clear the docks safely.

On arriving at Roscoff, Morlais was our first stop. We were going to try some French youth hostels as an experiment, but after Morlais YH decided they were not as good, or as well run as our YHAs in England, so it was to be camping from then on. We hoped there would not be too many campers in the field, as we had only put up the new tent once in the back garden, tent campers always love to watch someone else putting up a tent, especially on a windy day! They know the pitfalls, but they are always willing to help, they are a breed apart, but all went well, and the campsite, in the grounds of a chateau, was excellent.

The weather had improved the next morning and we cycled southwards through Quimper, to Fousnant and the Quiberon Peninsular, camping overnight at these places, then at Herbinac we turned northwards for the coast of North Brittany. Campsites were between 2 and 10 francs for two people a night. In ten days we had covered 320 km – 200 miles and it was time to go home. I will briefly list our route and campsites at the back of the book, if you are interested.

In 1978 Rog and Pam were married; the wedding was in Gloucester with families and friends present. We were very happy for them. Roger's job was now with the CEGB — Central Electricity Generating Board. In the same year and month, we had completed an agreement with Mr Peckett to buy Westhayes Cottage from him. We were now the proud owners of a nice house, and a now presentable garden, created from the overgrown piece of land when we first moved in.

The sense of freedom of the open road was now firmly established in our minds. Touring in this country, we cycled to the nearest railway station, and with the cycles in the guard's van, we 'drop off' the train further along the rails to explore pastures new. The guard's van, then, was quite large, and only about half-full with parcels, mail bags, boxes of baby chicks, dead rabbits or pheasants etc. The bicycles were attached securely to the side of the van, the station master checked, and then it was only a case of finding yourself a seat in one of the other carriages. Destination arrived, we saddled up, and were once more on the road to new and unexplored territory.

On all of these cycling tours in this country we used youths hostels for overnight stops, we were able to plan the whole journey in advance, could have a hot meal in the evening there, or cook our own in the members' kitchen. There were at least four tabletop cookers, cutlery and crockery available

Unfortunately, when the new trains were introduced some years ago, the guard's van disappeared, and only two bicycles per train were allowed, and then only in such a small cubicle provided, which made travelling with our cycle panniers prohibitive, the train could obviously not accommodate them, but from 1983 to 1994 they had served us well; we missed them.

Not to be deprived of our adventures, we bought two medium-sized back packs, and took to walking some lovely areas in this country of ours. The Lake District was a great favourite, where there are some fine youth hostels within reasonable walking distance of each other (8-10 miles). With stout shoes and a good map, it is comparatively easy walking across the hills and unbeaten track, and these days, no problem — with a mobile you can't get lost.

Of the times of which I am writing, we were just relying on our good spirits, a good map and intuition. We were in our 60s. Have a go! Don't be put off by the word *youth* hostel — they are for any age group. Unfortunately, some of the more inaccessible ones are being closed, because they are not being used enough, and more money is being spent on updating more popular ones. The times, they are a-changing! The old ones off the beaten track had charm, and sanctuary, after a long ride or walk. But we move with the times, and providing you can sleep on a bunk bed — family rooms, or two-bunk rooms are available — a youth hostel is very well run, and far better than many hotels, and in some lovely locations.

Sue married Adrian in 1980. We were so glad she would no longer be on her own. She sold her flat and together they bought a house in Surrey, near Dorking, which was suitable for Adrian's mum to have her own separate part of the house. We were very happy for Sue.

Looking back to 1984, what a year it was for camping! Easter at Coombe Martin, May Day at Torrington (Devon) and June saw us on the banks of the River Loire at Saumer in France, several days of cycling in the area was memorable for the heady perfume of roses which seemed to grow and blossom everywhere in profusion, and the smell of lime blossom was unmistakable and lovely, the little country roads took us through acres of sunripe strawberry fields and had the air of a cauldron of hot homemade strawberry jam, then there was the taste of sparkling Saumer wine, the sparkle naturally produced in the surrounding caves. A few weeks later at a camp site at Hay on Wye and Rhadirmwyn in Wales, the hills around were wild and beautiful, we saw our first sighting of a red kite there; moving back towards home, a farm campsite at Aberbran near Brecon is definitely recommended at mushroom time where the farmer told us to help ourselves, there were so many in the field we couldn't believe our eyes. Happy days!

As happened quite often, I saw a picture of a place I liked and painted it, hoping I would go there one day. This happened with a picture of the Tissington Trail. Enough said, we were off again! The Tissington Trail is in the Derbyshire Dales. Back packs at the ready, we walked the trail, through Dovedale, finishing at the village of Tissington, which was lovely. Our night stops were at Bakewell, Hartington, 11am Hall YHA, finishing with Buxton and Matlock. It was good.

Cycle camping tours continued. The Loire Valley was a great favourite, each tour branching out in a different direction, down the many tributary rivers, off the Loire, the Cher, Indre and Charant.

There was an early morning train from Caen to Tours that carried bicycles. Tours was a good jumping-off point for the River Loire or Saumer. One interesting tour was helped along by a new train service from Boulogne to the South of France, stopping at Brive, in which a special coach for carrying bicycles was attached to the train. The fare for cyclist and bicycle was £120 return. We liked the sound of that, because it would take us further south than our usual range. It was an all night journey; the bicycles were encased in cardboard containers, and wheeled away to their own carriage, and we made our way with pannier bags to a carriage with six double-decker bunks, and the train moved off in the fading light.

I dozed fitfully and some hours later the train came to a halt with a lot of clanking sounds, almost as if we were shunting into a siding; the wait was for about half an hour, then we moved off again. It was quite dark; slowly the dawn broke and the surrounding countryside began to appear — we were nearly there. Our destination was Brive as we hoped to tour the area around the Dordogne. Apart from the 20 cyclists and their bicycles, many passengers and their cars disembarked as well here. To our surprise, the station platform was arrayed with trestle tables laden with filled baguettes, coffee and biscuits. It was unexpected and unbelievable, but to our surprise, was part of the whole package, included in our fare; our hosts were very welcoming. Well fed, we prepared for the road again. There was one slight problem — several passengers, including some of our group of cyclists, had been robbed during the night; one cyclist had his only pair of shoes for the journey taken. Fortunately another cyclist lent him a pair of sandals until he was able to buy some in the town of Brive. It was thought the thieves had come aboard when the train was in the siding for half an hour. There was a lock on the carriage door, but obviously not often used. Beware!

It was a very enjoyable 14-day tour, incorporating the areas around Veyrac, Vers, Figeac, Roquamoder, St Cere and Agentat. At St Cere there was a holiday meet with the camping club (of Great Britain) — all caravans of course. They were intrigued how we carried everything on our bicycles. Horace stiffened his 'bell ends' with pride. The caravanners gathered around in the morning to watch us decamp and saddle up, and gave us a cheer as they waved us off. We were making our way back to the railway station at Brive and had some more good campsites on the way. Arriving at the station, the trestle tables were laid out as before, with food. We asked for the cardboard boxes for the bicycles we had had on the way down. They were not available, then a loudspeaker announced, in no uncertain terms, 'No breakfast for velos,' (bicycles). As a combined group of cyclists, en masse, we took this up with the station master, but he was adamant — 'No breakfast for velos.' All of us were of the same opinion — they could stuff their breakfast! On our return to England we took the matter up with the French railways, as a matter of principle. Many apologies later, and a refund from the French railways, it appears it was a big mistake by the station master at Brive. *Vive entente cordial!* I don't think the train service is running now, which is a pity, as it was good.

We now had three grandchildren: Two boys — Andrew and Richard — for Rog and Pam, a little girl — Joanna — for Sue and Adrian. It was lovely to meet up with them, go on walks, sail their boats in the large pools left by the tide at Sidmouth, catch little crabs and creatures in the rock pools. We loved them dearly.

In 1991 on one tour in Brittany, we knew they were holidaying in the caravan at Port L'epine; they didn't know we were in France. We decided to surprise them if we could get there. We would try.

After three night camp stops there was one particularly wet site, where I got out of my sleeping bag during the night (don't ask questions!) The grass outside was quite long and wet, and when I got back into my sleeping bag, there was something very slimy keeping me company — two huge slugs, which I must have brought back in with me on my feet. In the morning a bag of lovely ripe peaches had been half-eaten and the culprits were still in the paper bag — the biggest, yellow-bellied slugs I have ever seen. We vowed never to go back to that campsite.

We were getting quite near our destination and it started to rain. We donned rain gear, which made us quite unrecognisable. We stopped to look at the roadmap — it must be the next turning left. Then, what should be coming out of the turning? Roger's car with the family aboard! He was looking across the road and half-recognised the bicycles, in his disbelief, he switched off the windscreen wipers to get a better look and pressed the horn instead. It was a wonderful meeting! They were on their way to pick up some provisions, so we said we would go on down to the campsite, put up our tent and see them later. We were able to get a pitch next to their caravan, and had just about put the tent up when they returned. The boys were delighted to see us and come inside our tent. Richard had bought us a packet of biscuits from his own pocket money as he thought we would be hungry. Pam and Rog made us a cup of tea, and we all sat around on the grass eating and drinking tea, then we had a meal with them in their caravan.

The next day we all went out in the car, had a nice meal out, and enjoyed the lovely scenery of the coastline, called the Emerald Coast. We packed up camp the next morning to start our return journey back to the ferry. Andrew was very interested as to how we were going to get everything back on to our bicycles. Roger said he would pile all our gear into the back of his car to at least take us to the top of the big hill out of the campsite. Andrew wanted to come with us but Roger said there was not enough room for him, but when it was time to go, he managed to squeeze himself into the back of the car. With a full load, we got to the top of the hill and a little way along the road, then we were disgorged from the car at a suitable spot, where we could lean the bicycles against a wall and load them up. Andrew watched every movement; he has turned out in later years to be a keen cyclist himself.

It was time to say our farewells, and we 'wobbled' off down the road, trying to wave for as long as we could; the first wheel turn of the laden camping gear bicycle is always a slight wobble whilst you stabilise. After three camp night stops, returning on a slightly different route, avoiding the 'sluggy' campsite, we returned to our first campsite at Carantec, which was on the outskirts of the town, and spent several days there, as the cliff walks were good. Roger had said they might come over and try to find us. The distance in the car would make it possible in a day. We were having coffee in a café on the street that leads into the town, and sure enough we saw his car go by, and we were able to find them easily in the square. Lots of excitement again — the boys wanted to see our campsite, so that was what we did. Then we gathered up some food for a picnic, and took them on the cliff walk that we liked so much. This took us to a sandy beach with rocks for climbing over, and also a dip in the sea. The water was quite cold that day; I didn't get many takers — just Andrew and myself — but there were some lovely seashells, which Richard collected. There was ice cream to follow, and a visit to a cafe for crepes, then we had to part company. It was another very good day.

The next morning it was market day in the town and the streets were a colourful show of fruit and vegetables and snails of all kinds. There were chickens roasting on spits, sausages sizzling in pans, baguettes, and bread of every description. Our ferry didn't go until the afternoon, so we bought a small spit-roasted chicken and took it to the beach, pulled the legs off and ate them for lunch. We washed our hands in the rock pools, and took the rest of the chicken home, well wrapped in a plastic bag. What we had also bought was a jar of the juices from the deep tray below the roasting chicken, which also contained peppers, onions and garlic; it was absolutely delicious!

We have had some very good tours in France.

I tried in my competitions, but could never win a car. I didn't learn to drive until I was 60, and even then seldom took over the driver's seat, which was a mistake. I was not getting any younger, but I was determined I must drive. I really wanted a reliable, uncomplicated 'old banger', so that I could take it out quietly each day, to regain my confidence. I knew I was not a danger to anyone else, as my road sense was good after years of cycling. I saw an advertisement in the local paper for a car for sale for £700. I rang the telephone number. Yes, it was in good condition — a good point, as I am not very mechanically minded! 'What type of car is it?' I asked, thinking I sounded professional, although actually it meant nothing to me. Did it have a special name, a personal name? Yes — Beanie, and it was green. I liked that, Beanie would be my good friend. I did not tell Ken. Why? Because he wouldn't think it was a good idea. I made an appointment to see Beanie, and had the cheque made out ready.

Ken had gone to Ottery on his bicycle. I didn't know exactly where the house was, but it wasn't very far away, and the only way to get to it was by bicycle. I set off. At the crossroads I turned right down a quiet, fairly steep country lane. Halfway down the hill, I needed to slow up a bit, I applied the brakes, and the wheels slid sideways as I skidded on the mud and wet leaves at the side of the road. I landed with a thump with the bicycle on top of me, I checked myself out — my leg was bleeding, there was mud on my face and jacket, but my right hand was not functioning properly. Something must be broken. There were no passing cars or people around. I decided it was no good sitting there, I must get up and get on with it. I could see a house at the bottom of the hill — perhaps someone was at home. Mounting my bicycle, I tried to ride but my right hand had no control over the brake. I managed to scuff to a standstill walking was the best option. The house was empty and being renovated, so I pressed on, A little further along there was the sign I was looking for, and a narrow road leading to a cluster of houses. Resting my bicycle in the hedge, I looked around. The next question was which one was Beanie's? A lady came out of one of the houses, and luckily it was the right house.

I apologised for being late and explained why. Things happened quickly then. Quite unknown to me, Beanie's owner was one of our local doctors from the medical centre in Ottery, and his wife was also a doctor. How lucky can you get!? They confirmed the wrist was probably broken, and put my arm in a sling, and some patches on my leg. I would have to go to Exeter Hospital A&E, but Beanie's owner would take me to Ottery Hospital first, to clean up and dress the gash on my leg, which must have been caused by the pedal. My bicycle was strapped on the back of his car and was dropped off at our house on the way home. Also, I left a note for Ken to say where I was.

At the Hospital in Ottery I was cleaned up, and Ken arrived to take me into Exeter A&E, where the break was confirmed and put in plaster. It was so kind of the doctor and his wife to take so much trouble for me — I was very grateful.

Beanie had been a long-time friend of his I believe, they would have kept him for me — but that would not have been fair to them, as I would be in plaster for six weeks. Also, Ken thought I didn't need one as there was a perfectly good car in the garage to use, but that's not quite the same! You win some, you lose some! I hope Beanie found a good home.

There are so many memories over the years. With just a thought, pictures in your mind will recall that memory: The grandchildren growing up at different stages in their young lives; weekends in Bella, the Dormobile; meeting up with Rog, Pam and the boys at Bantham, and buried treasure by the rocks — I wonder if there is any still there, under the sand, boys? Times with Sue, Adrian and Joanna at Robin Cottage, Surrey, on Joanna's birthdays; Christmas making paper chains, Joanna's first steps across the kitchen from Sue to my outstretched arms — it must have been all of three steps; catching falling rose petals underneath the rose arbour in our garden with her and her happy laugh; cricket on the beach until, as they grew stronger, we couldn't get them out — the ball was going for sixes and the fielders couldn't run as fast as they used to; rock pooling at Sidmouth, jumping the waves, kite flying by the River Otter and on Woodbury Common, catching falling leaves in the autumn, each with the promise of a happy day to come; meeting up with Sue, Adrian and Joanna to surprise them at St Brievals youth hostel at the end of their week's holiday.

Camping and back packing, Sue surprising me with a tap on the shoulder in a small supermarket in Broadstairs, we were back packing and planned to stay at the youth hostel there that night, they had travelled miles just to see us for the evening. I remember it as if it was yesterday; Roger turning up unexpectedly to surprise us at our hotel, on our return from a holiday abroad — it's the thought that counts. There is so much to wonder at in their childhood and beyond. Don't ever lose it.

One thing we looked forward to every year was the Sidmouth Folk Festival — it was not to be missed. There was music and dancing everywhere. Impromptu groups performing on the promenade, clog dancers, morris dancers from many different counties and some from abroad, groups of singers, Balalaika music group and individual amateurs, children and adults (some quite old!) playing their music just for the love of it. One year I bought a second-hand accordion from the festival marquee and when I got home, I sat cross-legged on the lawn with it and played a tune straight away. After all those years ago when I was a teenager, I could still remember. I was hooked again and loved it. I have since bought a brand new one, which gives me much pleasure. I would love to sit on the prom one day and play, if I had the nerve.

I have never lost my love of cycling and camping has been another great pleasure in our lives. The fresh, sweet smell of the tent with its covering of morning dew, and the damp crushed grass; looking out from the unzipped flap of the tent to the wakening world, whilst you wait for the kettle to boil on the Trangia for the early morning mug of tea. We have had our moments to test the faint-hearted: There was the night in Jersey of terrific thunderstorms and high winds holding on to the tent poles to stabilise the tent's structure, even though we were well pegged down, the tent was billowing like a ship in full sail, but we survived. The next morning revealed caravan awnings flattened and some tents in shreds.

One trip in France there was exceptionally high winds; we had just come off the 'flats' of the levees, where, with the strong wind behind us, there was scarcely any need to pedal, then a sharp turn to the right into the busy thoroughfare leading into Tours brought us into the full force of the wind. We were obliged to dismount for safety's sake when crossing the bridge over the River Loire, as the wind could have blown us into the path of the fast-moving traffic. Surmounting that problem and moving on, we had to alter direction again to make for the campsite. At the traffic lights, the now cross winds blew me off my bicycle! Fortunately there was no immediate traffic behind me. I was patched up by the garage mechanics across the road, who had seen what had happened, but they advised further treatment from the town's doctor, and said they would look after our bicycles. The doctor stitched me up and advised me to rest and no cycling for two days. It was a painful night in the sleeping bag! We returned to the garage for our bicycles and to thank them for their help. We had to get back to England that weekend for our Ruby Wedding celebrations when all the family were coming, so the next day we caught the train from Tours to Caen and the overnight Ferry home. We had a lovely time together. That's what I like about family gatherings — the feeling of being together, the fun and warmth is not to be missed.

Christmas is another time not to be missed. Whilst Sue, Adrian and Joanna were in Surrey, their time over the Christmas, of course, was spent with Adrian's mum. Joanna's birthday was in early December, and so every year we went to Robin Cottage for her birthday and then had a special Christmas dinner with them and Adrian's mum. Then we had another Christmas time with Roger, Pam, Andrew and Richard in Gloucester. Gran, Grandad and the boys on Christmas Eve sang carols in the hall for Rog and Pam. Then on Christmas evening, a special invitation was issued for Rog and Pam to be in their seats at 7.30, and the boys and ourselves entertained them. I have several books of funny poems, children's poems and Pam Ayres etc. The boys were able to pick their own poem from the books and were very good at reciting them. There were lots of jokes, which they did as a double act, and it was a lot of fun. They served chocolates to their parents afterwards.

After Adrian's mum died, Sue, Adrian and Joanna moved to Lydford and a house on the edge of Dartmoor with lovely views, and about 14 acres of land. It had several spare rooms and also one very large room, which looked out over the fields to the tors of Dartmoor. At Christmas time especially it leant itself perfectly to the festive season, with its wooden beams, very large log fire, and latticed windows. In the corner of the room a few steps led up to a small balcony overlooking the room below and led off into another room. A Christmas tree cut from the woods reached to the ceiling in the other corner of the room to complete the picture. Christmas decorations across the beams, and it was ready for Christmas.

The room acquired its name 'the secret room' right from the beginning. This was how it happened. Moving day arrived for Sue, Adrian, Joanna and Toby, their dog. The removal van had left and Sue and Adrian were to follow in their car. We had a phone call some time in the morning to say they had broken down and were waiting for a recovery vehicle to arrive — could we possibly go down to Lydford to see the furniture van and assist the furniture into place. We were soon ready; it takes about an hour to get to Lydford from here; there was no sign of the van first of all — I think they were having lunch. We obtained the keys from the previous owner, although he was not quite ready to go, but that having been sorted out, the van arrived and the furniture brought in. As we had not been in the new house before, items were being assigned where we thought best, and we breathed a sigh of relief when everything had been brought in. Then we saw another door, up a few stairs, and another door — lo and behold, there was this lovely big room, and from then on we have always called it the 'secret room.'

The recovery vehicle came quite soon afterwards, with Sue, Adrian and Joanna in the front cab, and their car on the trailer behind, with Toby, their dog, looking out of the window, quite mystified. We were able to make a cup of tea on the camping stove and help put up the beds as a temporary measure, and then we went home and returned the next morning to help finish the job.

We have been meeting there every Christmas ever since — the three families: Christmas Eve, Christmas Day, and Boxing Day. We know it cannot always be so — the grandchildren will get married and have families of their own and have other priorities. We will enjoy it whilst we can.

Chapter 10

In June we had a camping holiday at our favourite campsite, Trewan Hall, Nr Padstow, and a pleasant cycle ride along the Camel Trail. The following day was our annual walk along the estuary from Padstow. We had coffee overlooking the harbour, and then it was 'best foot forward' up the path that led to the war memorial, with lovely views across the estuary to Rock. Over the stile, or through the gate, depending on the state of your legs, and on to the coastal path. It was always our plan a little further along to leave the path and divert to the right when St George's Cove comes into view to clamber down some rocks to the sandy beach below — but take care!

Here we would take off our shoes and socks, tie the shoes by their laces to our belt, feel the gorgeous sense of warm sand between our toes, and go down to the incoming tide and the gently breaking waves — bliss! We then work our way along the beach, paddling through the water's edge, to the farthermost point of the beach and the rocks — sometimes to have a bathe, but always to have our sandwich lunch, sat on the rocks, with a 'brew up' on the Trangia for a mug of tea — what more could you ask? In other years we had always climbed back up to the coastal path at this point, which carries on along, via a steep climb to Stepper Point. Every year we wondered if we can still make it to the Point — this was 1997 and we were 77! Did we make it? Of course we did, and Ken has a handwritten certificate to prove it on the back of a Padstow Estuary postcard.

For several months, there had been limited building going on around Westhayes, where we had been used to green fields. There were still plenty of trees, but to be sure we decided to plant some smaller trees at the top of the garden to make a backdrop. We chose three white-barked silver birches, one rowan, an ornamental cherry and an Acer. They serve the purpose beautifully; I love trees. The garden is my pride and joy and gardening is the most relaxing thing I know. To grow something from a seed or cutting and produce plants of such beauty and diversity is amazing to me. The creation is not mine, but my part is the ability to nurture and make it possible, and then create a garden.

The next year we were to plan another tour in France, which included Tourneville, La Bagage, St Saviour and Jonville. The tour was shortened halfway round, when there was a loud crack from Ken's back wheel — a spoke had broken in the wheel. Ken carries most tools for cycle repair when we go on these trips, but this was a breakage that needed more detailed equipment. As we had left the previous small town, we had noted a cycle shop on the outskirts. We retraced our steps, walking of course. The owners of the bicycle shop were very helpful, saying they could repair the wheel in two hours. France is notably biased and friendly towards cyclists. We walked around the town, which was very pleasant, and when we returned, as promised the wheel was ready; it was a great relief. We had intended to cross over to the other coast of the peninsula, but as the country roads we take are sometimes quite far from civilisation, Ken thought it was best to make for home the way we had come until he was sure his bicycle would not have any more problems.

The weather was warm and the area pleasant as we ambled back along the quiet road to Tourneville and our previous campsite, which was quite small and a previous orchard, I should think. A party of young girls turned up soon after us, looking quite worn out and one hobbling painfully. When they passed our tent, I made some conversation with them. They were students on a walking trip, not very well equipped, and had blisters on their feet, the one girl especially. I offered to have a look, which was accepted, and it was bathed, cleaned up, and a blister patch put on, and one to take with her for the next day. The next morning she looked more comfortable as they left, which I was glad about.

We moved on the next day. It was still quite warm and we were looking for shade to have our midday picnic. We came across a travelling dream, it was a recently cut hay field — lovely, dry, and sweet smelling. After eating our French bread and cheese, I lay back in the hay with my sunhat over my face and had a ten-minute snooze — give me a grassy bank and some warm sun and I can do that anytime. This was dry, warm hay, even better, but then it was time to saddle up again and make for the next campsite.

After several days I felt a small lump on the back of my neck when I combed my hair. I couldn't see it so I conveniently forgot it; there was nothing I could do until I got home, where I asked Ken to have a look, he said he thought it was alive, and yes it was! I saw the doctor the next day — it was a tick. The doctor removed it there and then, and proudly showed me the creature on the end of his forceps with its legs still waving frantically, it was dark with the blood it had been feeding on from me for four days. Because of the time I had been carrying it, I had to watch out for a red area forming on my neck, as ticks can introduce something nasty into the blood. The red mark around the spot did appear, and I had to have the area around of flesh removed, and stitched up. As to where the tick came from? I think there is a moral to this story — don't snooze in a hayfield!

Through the intervening years, thoughts would surface from the back of my mind concerning the continuity of life and the family Ken and I had built up. What made me tick? What kind of genes had been passed on? Who was I like? I knew about Dad's family, but nothing really about mum. My thoughts were stirred and brought back pictures in my mind of people I had known in Frenchay, my village from 1920 to my entry into the WAAF 1941/2. I decided to try and research Mum's family, and in the process, my own.

What were the known facts? Dad's words to me in 1935 sprang to mind — ie 'Gran is not your real gran.' My grandfather was an artist who travelled abroad a lot. This I felt was on the right track, and one gene that had been passed down. I had had a feeling one day several years before to paint and, using some old watercolour tubes of paint Sue had left behind, I drew and painted from one of the many photographs we had taken in the past. I found it effortless and rewarding to produce a watercolour picture and I never looked back; the walls of our house are festooned with paintings of where we have been through the years. It was a small needle in a big haystack, but something to build on.

Another incident came to mind: Once a year Granfer Mann would come up to our house in the January for Dad to write out Sutton's Seeds' list for Mr Fry's garden. Dad's handwriting was excellent, and a pleasure to see. When they had completed the list, Dad and Granfer would adjourn to the White Lion, a few houses away, where after a few pints the conversation flowed. Dad seldom saw Granfer on his own in such circumstances, and I suppose it was the opportunity to talk things over and slip in a few questions, but Granfer didn't seem to know a lot, except that Mum had asked Gran to contact her real mum when I was born in 1920. Gran had said no, it wasn't possible. He also said the ten shillings a week paid to Gran for fostering Mum stopped after two years, as such, but other arrangements had been made. Now, how did that tie in? He did mention a name I had heard from Aunt Edie, as I have said earlier. Once again, I had put it at the back of my mind, but this time I paid a little more attention. I didn't recognise the name, it was no one I knew. Mum had been brought as a baby in 1895 to Mrs Mann at Frenchay and was fostered by her, that much I knew for certain.

I did some researching into the Mann family. It seemed they originally worked as housekeeper and gardener to a Mr Ward who lived at the Grange, Northwoods. Four daughters were born to them in the cottage adjoining the grange — Edith, Ada, Lilly and Hilda. In 1894, Mr Ward and his sister moved to Riverwood, Frenchay, where Granfer continued to work for them there as gardener. The same year, the Mann family moved to Frome Villas, Frenchay, owned by the Tucketts. Riverwood was formerly occupied by Philip Tuckett. In 1916, the Wards moved to a house on the Common, and Riverwood was purchased by Cecil Fry and his young family, Barbara, David and Jeremy, that we knew well in our young days.

I browsed in libraries and read a lot about Victorian times, biographies and autobiographies, which led me to many snippets of information, and many journeys to archives further afield, where letters from the past gave me useful insights into the times they lived in, in and around the 1890s. I was fascinated by the written words preserved from the distant past in handwritten letters; I doubt if this will apply to our times, when email is the 'in thing'. The letters gave me food for thought.

I contacted Mum's stepsister in London, the only one still alive. Aunty Lilly said she knew very little, but whatever the circumstances of her fostering, Mum had more than repaid them by caring for Gran, Granfer and Aunt Edie in all their later lives. One thing she did also mention was that Hilda (stepsister) and Mum were to have been confirmed together, but someone in the village objected about Mum being confirmed as May Mann, as that was not her real name. This was the first Mum had known she had been fostered, and she was very upset; she asked Gran who her real mother was. Gran was very cross that Mum should have found out in that way, and said, 'Your mother was a wicked woman — you don't want to know, never ask about her again.' It left a lasting impression on Mum, I am sure.

I have thought about Gran's words 'your mother was a wicked woman'. Gran was of moral stock, Methodist chapel, and Quaker meetings, and the implications of the word 'wicked' was the fact that the child Mum's mother bore, she had given away, not wicked as in stealing or being untruthful — it was a dishonour in Victorian times to have a child out of wedlock and abandon it, even if there was no choice. But it was quite common for the wealthy to have children outside marriage. A son was important to a wealthy family and was cosseted as heir to the family name and business. Strangely enough, the sons were not always strong and healthy. Extra girl offspring were often absorbed into the family nurseries of the wealthy, and brought up with the other children by nursemaids and governesses, and with little education, thus avoiding the scandal for the master or mistress of the house. If that was inconvenient, they were farmed out to known retainers, who could keep secrets, never knowing their parentage. There was a big divide between those who had money and those who had not.

The Confirmation episode left a big void in Mum's life, but she was strong-minded, outspoken and fiercely independent, sometimes haughty, but very caring of old people, and a great lover of animals. She wasn't outwardly affectionate — I think she found that difficult. Maybe it was a form of defence. As children, we were brought up to be good mannered and good citizens, but mainly to be independent, and to get on with whatever life presented us with; there was no pampering.

Mum was very good looking and had wonderfully strong brown hair, which went completely white at the age of 40. She was so unlike her sisters, and anyone else in the village. She loved dancing and Old Time dances. At the village hall dances, the younger generation would sit around in groups, not joining in, purely because they had never mastered the quite intricate steps of the Boston two step, Waltz, Veleeta etc. It came about that Mum completely cleared our end bedroom, installed the gramophone, and invited all the young people to come and learn the steps, lemonade and biscuits provided. The word spread and about eight girls turned up — no boys — but a good time was had by all over several sessions. The girls learned quickly and could join in the dances, even if they had girl partners, not the best of options, but that was as it was. The boys, as ever, hung about in clusters by the door, but it was all good fun — social occasions are an essential part of village life.

I went back one day to my village of Frenchay, where Mum had lived her life, until Mum and Dad came to live with us in their last years. There were very few of the older inhabitants left from those times, bearing in mind that I myself was in my 60/70s and the memories of those left were as passed down from their parents. Miss Elliot could remember being told by her mother that she had seen the horse-drawn carriage travelling along the old coach road, bringing Mum as a baby in 1895, accompanied by nursemaid and coachman, stopping briefly as it turned off the Common, for Frenchay Hill. Louise Powell's mother lived opposite Frome Villas, where Mrs Mann and family lived, and remembers the horse-drawn carriage bringing Mum as a baby accompanied by a nursemaid to Mrs Mann. All the village probably knew that much by teatime, but the secret from then on was always safe with Mrs Mann. Having four older sisters was a good environment for a new baby to come into. I was told also that Mrs Mann was the local midwife, but I am not sure if this was true.

It was quite nostalgic to be back in Frenchay again. The village itself had not altered, and never will. The old cottages have been renovated. The Post Office, where Barbara had lived — and which she eventually took over from her mother as post mistress — had closed down, as also had Mrs Baber's grocery shop, the bakery and the shop selling paraffin and candles; all dead and gone. But the Common will always remain, as will the large houses that line the road down to Gran's, now old, bungalow, St Hilary, and Beck's Pool; it will always be a conservation village. Any new houses on the village perimeter have, on the whole, been quite tastefully done.

My thoughts were stirred, and brought back to my mind people I had known there. Yes, it was a good place to grow up in, and people were good to us. Mrs McGregor Fry visited Esme, my sister, every week during her long illness with rheumatic fever, bringing her little gifts such as small china animals, and a small round tin of solid perfume inside, the perfume being released by rubbing your warm finger on it. It's strange how these little memories remain. Mrs Tuckett was very good to Mum, and for her wedding she gave her a light oak bedroom suite, with a marble top washstand, and a drop-leaf dining table with a curved, central leg and wide clawed feet, also, at some time, she was given by her a 20-garnet broach which Esme now has. Gran and Granfer of course, had the new bungalow built for them.

Of the daughters, Mum's stepsister Ada went to Australia and married there. Lily and Hilda went into service in the larger houses of London. Edith always stayed at home because of her deafness and increasing blindness. Mum was apprenticed to Jolly's of Bristol as a seamstress. Gran and Granfer continued to live in the bungalow and Mum was able to look after Gran and do their shopping.

With research I found that Rose Cottage had been sold to Mrs Mann in 1928, for X number of pounds — that's the year we moved into Rose Cottage. Now, Gran didn't have this amount of money on Granfer's wages. Gran 'sold' it to Mum for X number of pounds — I have seen the deeds. I know Mum didn't have that amount of money. I think it could have been one of the 'other arrangements'. My researching was improving.

Libraries are like Aladdin's cave, and full of written gems from the past and little smidgens of knowledge for the future, and so it was I came across such spoken words from the past that were of such interest to me. There were also two authors I wished to contact. I found that one had died, but the other confirmed her writings and admitted she should have followed up certain comments at the time, but thought it inappropriate and had not done so. I could — and would — follow them up. There were sufficient notes to lead me Northwards. The names now are fictitious. I have no wish to cause displeasure to any descendants still alive.

I caught the train north to York, and stayed overnight, arranging for a 6am taxi to take me to the station, and a further connection the next morning. Alighting at my destination at that early hour, the station was quite deserted with no station master. I took the only exit from the station, which led to a wider main road, but there was no signpost or traffic about. I took pot luck, turned left and kept walking, not a car or person passed me.

I came to a fork in the road, which one should I take? To the left, there were at least some houses in the distance. Then, joy of joys, a postman on a bicycle! I caught up with him and asked if he could tell me please if I was on the right road to Barmouth? 'Not on this road, but if you follow those school children down the right-hand lane, they will be going to the town.' he said I did, and finally arrived at 8.30am. The shops were not open yet. One hotel showed signs of life — a group of residents were gathering outside; maybe a coach party.

I continued on until I reached the open grassland, overlooking the beach. It was a pleasant, calm morning, but beachcombing was not my plan for the day. I retraced steps to the 'shop closed' main street. Through the open hotel door, I saw the guests were having coffee in the lounge. I felt like joining and mingling with them — the coffee smelt good, but a few doors away a newsagent's was opening up; there was a small elderly lady in charge, I approached her and opened up a conversation, on the possibility that she might sell chocolate. She did so I bought some, and then asked casually if there was a bus service, she replied there was one that ran infrequently. Was there a taxi service? I asked. 'No,' she replied, 'there used to be one, we kept the notice in the window for some time but I don't remember the number.' She thought for a minute. 'The advert may still be around.' She rummaged in the drawer. 'Yes, it's here.' I thanked her and made a note of the number.

There was a telephone across the road — should I cross the road and take a chance? There really was no choice. To fail now, after coming all this way, was not an option. I rang the number. The taxi driver said he would be about 20 minutes. I ate my chocolate. A car drew up, not exactly the top of the range, driver youngish, sleeves rolled up, but cheery. I got in the car with some misgivings, but thought of my trusty folding sheath knife I use for camping, but always carry with me in my pocket on my 'away from home' journeys. I told him my destination, where I would stop for half an hour, and asked if he could return there in half an hour to pick me up and take me back to the station, to catch the train to York. The taxi driver said that would be all right, as he had an uncle in the said village who he would call on for half an hour. Being local, he knew my destination. I was quite surprised.

I arrived safely. The house was quite large and solidly built. I went to the back of the house and rang the bell. What was I going to say?! A young girl answered the door. I asked for Captain Hopton, and she said she would fetch him. In a few minutes an elderly gentleman came to the door, accompanied by three dogs barking their heads off. The young girl rounded them up, explaining they had just been fed, and were quite harmless. Captain Hopton closed the door behind him to calm them down. I told him my name and who I thought my grandfather was and that I was inquiring into the possible connection with his family, and what it might be. He was intrigued, interested, and not at all surprised. He told me quite a bit about his grandmother and cousin Evelyn — both of whom were of interest to me — her interest in horses and singing, and more strangely, his cousin Evelyn would sometimes spend nights out in a tent in their field with her dog, communicating by carrier pigeon with the house when she wanted food brought to her. He said he couldn't ask me in as the dogs would create such a noise.

My half-hour was nearly up. In my last few minutes there, I asked him about some diaries written by his grandmother. Did he know about them and were they still in existence? He knew about them, but they were not now in his possession, they had been lent to his cousin. My time was up. He asked for my name and address, then I hurried across the courtyard to look for my taxi. It was already there and waiting; his uncle had been out, unfortunately, but he was quite unperturbed.

Back at the railway station, there was now a station master in attendance, and an hour to wait for my train back to York, and then home — mission accomplished. It had been interesting. I thought that would be the end of it, but no! I had a letter from Captain Edward Hopton three days later, apologising for being so ungallant, and not asking me in, but to please return, as he had so much to show me in the house, and would like to meet me again. It was a moment to savour. I would be back as soon as the occasion and home life allowed.

About three months elapsed before I could manage another trip 'up north', but eventually it was arranged that I would be there at the house at ten o'clock. The house was called Northwood. I made arrangements beforehand, with a local taxi in that area to pick me up from the station and take me to Northwood House, and I would call him by phone, when I had finished my appointment, to return me to my accommodation in Wickham, where I was booked in for the night. I had no idea how long I would be; I had an overnight stop at York youth hostel for the previous night, because York was a convenient place for getting an early morning train connection for my ten o'clock appointment. Arrangements were made for an early morning taxi to collect me, and take me to York Station.

I was awake early and ready to go. My abode for the night slept on while I waited at the entrance — the minutes ticked by and nothing came. The staff were by now opening up and asked if they could help? They tried several other taxis, and, with only five minutes to spare, one took me at breakneck speed to the station. I raced up the steps and across the bridge, only to see my train pulling out of the station. I stood looking over the bridge, I could not believe my well laid plans had gone awry. A railway man going off duty said, 'What's up? Missed the train? Where are you going? Don't worry, there's a commuter train going part of your way on the next platform, and you can get a connection from there.' From dejection to exhilaration! I was down to that platform in a flash and boarding the train. It was packed with commuters, but who cares? I was on my way again.

It was about 80 miles on the commuter train to its destination and we arrived at nine o'clock. The next hurdle was to get a train to take me further on, but there was no connection that would get me to my destination at anywhere near my appointed time. There was a taxi rank outside of the station with a small office and two helpful girls in charge. Could they find me a reliable taxi? Ah! They didn't think so, as all the available taxis were out and it would be a 25-mile journey. With a little more discussion amongst themselves, they thought maybe 'Jim' would do it, but it would be 20 minutes before he would be back in the rank. It was my only chance. I waited, literally tapping the minutes away with my foot.

Jim turned up driving a London taxi. I slid thankfully into the capacious back seat. Jim was a pleasant young man. He knew my destination and said, 'Well, sit back on your seat and relax, we will get you there.' I realised I was perched on the edge of my seat with clenched hands, but I did try to calm down. When I had arrived at my last station I had rung my previously arranged taxi to explain I would not now be on the originally planned York train, but would compensate him for his wasted time when he collected me from Northwood House later in the day. He didn't mind.

By now we were approaching the long drive to the house. Something I hadn't noticed on my previous visit was that the drive divided as we neared the house — now, which should we take? The right was decided; the last time I had arrived at the back of the house, but very soon I was looking across a vast lawn to long windows at the front of the house. Could someone be looking out of those windows in amazement at this London taxi invading their space? Ah well, at least I was here, albeit half an hour late for my appointment — not a good start.

I rang the front door bell and waited, then rang again. A middle-aged lady came to the door and said, 'Oh yes, you are expected, come in.' The front door led into a large conservatory, which stretched along the front of the house. It was full of lovely plants, which created a moist, green scented atmosphere, and quite unusually a climbing geranium spread its blooms about 12ft up the connecting wall of the house. Well-worn mellow stone steps from either side led up to a stone balcony to another door, which we entered. The lady asked me to take a seat, and said she would tell Captain Hopton I was there.

In a few minutes Mrs Hopton came in and shook hands, and asked me if I would like some coffee. I was in a very large room with long vertical windows overlooking the lawn and beyond; there were large oil portraits on all the walls.

Captain Hopton entered the room followed by his wife with coffee and freshly made shortbread biscuits. From there on the conversation flowed freely and easily; they were not at all surprised at my questions. I sipped my coffee and nibbled my biscuit. I had to accommodate my crumbly shortbread biscuit carefully, in case it was my turn to speak. In the end, I quietly slipped it in my pocket just in case. They were friendly and easy to talk to and I felt at ease. His name was Edward and his wife, Grace. Edward showed me around the house, and explained who some of the portraits were of. There was one very large painting, which stretched the length of one wall in the Hall. It had been painted by his grandfather, and was of Venice, where they had been on holiday. He mentioned the diaries of his grandmother, which he had lent to his cousin when his aunt died, and said he would try and see where they were. Grace asked me if I would like to stay for lunch, but I thought it best to decline, to let them think things over, and asked if I could ring for my taxi.

Edward took me to the phone in his study. Once again the walls were covered in portraits, one painted by Andrew Kane of a portrait of his brother, which had been drafted on one of his visits to Northwood. Andrew was an excellent portrait painter, but he always strove endlessly to improve his landscapes. It was the vogue in the 1800 to 1900s to have your portrait painted and then framed quite ornately.

My taxi was due in 15 minutes and the time passed quickly. With the large rooms and long corridors, it was difficult to hear the doorbell, but investigating a faint sound we found the taxi waiting. The driver had not rung again because he had been trying to extricate the family cat, quite a young one, which had crept under his car, and wouldn't come out! That was soon put right, and the taxi took me to Wickham, and my accommodation for the night, collecting me the next morning, for the station, and my journey home.

A letter came a few days later saying they had enjoyed my visit, and would like me to come again.

Chapter 11

My next visit was in November 1997. My plans progressed without complications this time. I booked into a different guest house. The first stop was York as usual. Ken was coming with me, and intended to explore the little side streets of York, whilst I was travelling further north. We stayed in York that night and I caught the early train the next morning; this gave me time to drop off my holdall and check over the guest house. My appointment was for 11am at Northwood House.

I was welcomed when I arrived and we had coffee in the conservatory. They were still very interested in my life and story, of course, and I found them very easy to talk to. Afterwards, the conservatory plants were closely looked at, and named, some species had been brought from abroad many years ago; the geranium was amazing, I feel bound to mention it again — it blended so well with the stone steps, its blooms winding upwards, possibly 30 or more. We moved back into the house to look at some portraits on the wall, and ascertain who they were; there was a small picture on the wall by the window, Grace thought I looked like one of the two girls — they were Edward's cousins.

It was time for the dogs to be taken for their daily walk, there were about eight of them. Grace knew the pedigree of each one of them and had exhibited the breed in earlier days. Edward took them out every day and asked me if I would like to join him. It was a regular way every day, across the lawn and down some steps, then through a little gate to join the drive, bordered by trees and shrubs, planted for different occasions in their life. Edward loved the place, and would always look after it, and keep it in the family.

Lunch was ready when we returned, and passed pleasantly. As it came to an end, Edward told me to look over to the corner of the room, as there was something for me. Standing on an artist's easel was a large oil painting of a young lady. It was a beautiful head and shoulders portrait of Evelyn as a young girl painted by an Italian artist.

I didn't quite know what to say, I was overwhelmed, but was able to convey my extreme pleasure. We retired to the drawing room, and talked a lot more. My taxi arrived as arranged to take me back to Wickham, and the driver sounded his horn. Edward couldn't move very fast, so he told me to go on ahead and cancel it as he would take me to Wickham later. I apologised to the driver, and arranged for him to pick me up from the guest house the next morning, and told him I would settle up with him for his wasted journey. In the meantime, Grace had put a large cardboard container around the painting to protect it and make it easier to carry. It was quite light, as it was without picture frame. Grace, Edward and myself had much else to talk about and an hour later Edward drove me to Wickham and deposited the painting and myself in the hall of my guest house.

Early the next morning the taxi dropped me at the railway station to catch the through train to Exeter, stopping at York. Ken was on the platform and joined me there. The first seat by the door of the carriage conveniently had a space behind my seat which accommodated my painting. Ken had had a good day in York the day before, browsing through the old streets, and having coffee and lunch at 'Betty's'. They make very good coffee there, not to be missed if you are in York. We were on our way home again with many memories and things to think about.

In the months between, several visits were made to the archives at Ambridge, where the archivist was very helpful. I really enjoyed being in such an ancient establishment — it's so important they exist.

Cycling and motor caravanning continued; we had exchanged Bessie for another Dormobile, as Bessie's 'petticoats' had got very rusty, partly because she could not be garaged, her height being the problem. Our next VW had a better arrangement for cooking and sleeping and we called her Bella. Many happy days and weekends at Trewan Hall near Padstow were spent in her.

Grace had rung me to say they now had the diaries in their possession, which I could see whenever I was next their way. This was great news. I liked Edward and Grace and thought I would like to meet other members of the Evelyn family, cousins of Edward, if they were willing to meet me. I rang Kathleen, Evelyn's eldest granddaughter, and arranged a meeting at her convenience on my next trip to the north. On this journey, I continued on into Scotland, where Kathleen met me on the railway station, and took me back to her bungalow. We got on very well and talked of her grandmother Evelyn and great grandmother Lucy, and the friendship over the years which had developed between them and Andrew Kane, that indeed had lasted for the rest of their lives. Kathleen had a watercolour hanging on her wall by Andrew, a landscape of the area in the South of France where the Hopton's family home was and so many happy times had been spent there by Evelyn and Andrew. A sketch of Lucy was done there which met with approval from the family, and Andrew was commissioned to do a full-length oil painting of her. Quite a lot of the painting was portrayed at her grandmother's house in Lancashire and her sister's house and garden in Wales.

Kathleen had a small autograph book in which Evelyn had written at the time:

Oh that it were possible, after long grief and pain,
To find the arms of my true love around me once again.

That evening Kathleen and I made a framework of a plan. We would travel together to the South of France the next summer, to see if the family home still existed, and walk around the old small town in the footsteps of Lucy, Evelyn and Andrew, to see what they had seen, and feel the atmosphere of days gone by. But that dream was not to be. I broke my wrist when I came off of my bicycle in early spring, and later that year Kathleen was not able to. These things happen, but I would still like to do it.

The next morning Kathleen took me to the station to catch an early morning train south, and later I arrived at Wickham, where I was booked into a hotel. In the afternoon I hired a mountain bicycle and rode the six miles to Northwood, where Edward and Grace were expecting me and the diaries were laid out on the bureau, ready for me. After coffee, Edward took the dogs for their usual walk, leaving me to browse through the diaries sitting on the windowsill of one of the long windows overlooking the lawn. I chose the months and years in Lucy's diary that were of interest to me. I could only scan the surface of their contents in the short time, and I wondered if I could possibly ask Edward if I could take one home, but I need not have worried as Grace had already asked him if I could, and he had agreed; also that I could take two of the other diaries as well — one written by Evelyn from her childhood. I was overjoyed.

It was lunchtime, and all too soon time to be leaving my reading. But I looked forward to lunch, which now we always had in their large kitchen, by mutual arrangement. A ploughman's type lunch was the favourite with tasty cheese and sliced ham, and on this day, followed by strawberry sponge cake, from their own strawberries. It was very homely. Soon after lunch, Edward had to leave to go down to the strawberry fields, where every year his regular customers came to pick strawberries for strawberry jam. Grace and I talked awhile and I arranged to pick them up for an evening meal at our hotel. I packed the precious diaries in my backpack, and cycled back to the hotel, where Roger had already arrived. I had a room for him, he had been on business on the West coast, and had travelled across. We had a pot of tea and a walk around the town before returning to Northwood House for Edward and Grace, and a very enjoyable evening with them. Roger and I travelled back to Gloucester the next morning, where I continued by train to Exeter and home.

The following days at home, I found the diaries immensely interesting in the years I was researching. Quite strangely, all of Lucy's and her children's diaries finished on 6th May 1894 — something traumatic must have happened around that day. I made my notes as quickly as possible. I felt very responsible for the diaries, and carefully wrapping them in padded Post Office bags, I returned them to Edward by registered post.

By piecing together the researching in the Ambridge archives and the contents of the diaries, I was able to build up a picture in my mind of Lucy, Evelyn and Andrew. I will take you back 100 years. It was 1891. The three met on holiday in Florence, Italy, and then again at the family home in the South of France, where Andrew joined them.

Lucy was the daughter of a 'well to do' Victorian Family, and the first-born. The offspring of such families were placed in the care of a nursemaid, and later a governess. They were brought to see their mother for an hour before bedtime, when Mother would most probably read them a story and kiss them goodnight before returning them to the nursemaid. The governess in Lucy's case, and in the early days, was lacking in kindness and basic education, but had been taken on by Lucy's mother on the recommendation of her mother-in-law, who was not to be gainsaid.

In time, Lucy was joined by three sisters and a brother. A son was considered the important member of the family, to carry on the family name. When it was found the son was also being mistreated, the governess was dismissed immediately. The new governess was kind and they all loved her, and with her limited knowledge, she taught them all she knew.

Growing up in Wales Lucy had little contact with other companions of her own age, and when the family moved to Gayton House, on the death of her grandfather, at the age of 14 a new world opened up for her, but where she felt shy and uneducated in the social graces when she visited her mother's parents and they entertained. She had grown beautiful, and a suitor asked the family if he might call. The family agreed, but on the first visit, it was a shy, stilted occasion, and her sisters had to be always present. Nevertheless, after several months when he was away on business, he returned, and his offer of marriage was accepted by Lucy.

After the wedding, they returned to Northwood House to start life together. Lucy wanted desperately to improve her knowledge. She was a quick learner and Herbert a patient teacher; he was greatly interested in antiquities and Lucy accompanied him on a journey by steamer to explore the Nile — this was before the source of the Nile had been discovered. Lucy enjoyed the basic accommodation and the contact with the native population, making friends, treating minor injuries from her medical chest and learning the language.

Herbert was away on business for long stretches, mainly in Ireland, and she missed the company of her sisters. It was a happy marriage, born of respect, but not love, she was to say in later years.

When on holiday in Italy, Lucy and Evelyn met an aspiring English artist in Florence, Andrew Kane, and they became firm friends. Evelyn was Lucy's second daughter. The three of them — Lucy, Evelyn and Andrew — met many times during the following months and years on their return to England and at their holiday home in the South of France.

Evelyn and Andrew were more than half in love, but they were two very different characters. Evelyn loved horses and racing hard across the moor with her dogs and hawk; she loved singing and acting on the stage. She was beautiful and headstrong, and had many admirers, I think unconsciously she was a flirt, and was therefore misunderstood by some young men and some older men, who should have known better. Her parents wanted a good marriage for their daughter, as her elder sister had done. Evelyn was her father's favourite and Lucy kept a watchful eye on the possible suitors, but considered Andrew a safe friend; she quite liked Andrew herself.

Andrew was from a family with very strong religious beliefs, and with a charitable background. Their beliefs were sustained in most cases by intermarriages with like-minded families. These beliefs Andrew was questioning, especially when he conversed with his university friends who were always ready for a good debate. He could always make up his own mind, but still some of the old restrictions ran through his blood. He had chosen to follow his desired subject, Art, against his parents' wishes; their choice for him was science, which he was very good at.

Andrew and Evelyn continued to meet in the next few years in spite of a few love affairs by Evelyn, which she openly wrote about in her many letters. In spite of their differences, Andrew was very attracted to Evelyn and she was his first love. The inevitable happened and Andrew proposed marriage to her. Of course, it came to Lucy's attention and Evelyn's father was furious. He thought Andrew was a struggling artist with no future for his daughter. Lucy went to see Andrew, to tell him that Evelyn would ruin his career as an artist. So it came about that he was banned from the house, and from seeing her. There was much unhappiness, and sadly Evelyn turned down his offer of marriage.

Lucy continued to write to him, as she said she didn't intend to be deprived of a friend. Evelyn decided to make something of her idle lifestyle, as Andrew called it, and applied for a nursing position in a leading London hospital. In 1894 she was accepted. Andrew was living in London and the friendship was renewed. Meanwhile Lucy continued to correspond with him. He was beginning to make a name for himself in the art world and also as an art critic.

Herbert had agreed to buy the full-length portrait of Lucy, when finished but something happened, and the finished portrait came to light many years later when Andrew moved house. I wonder why?

Hospital did not suit Evelyn, and she left early in 1895 to take over Home Farm, part of the estate. In 1899 she married a wealthy landowner. It was not a happy marriage. Andrew married but his wife's untreatable illness saddened and marred his life. The years that had gone before were never forgotten, and they remained close friends until the end — Evelyn, Andrew and Lucy.

Two worlds had collided with the inevitable consequences. Any other way than the one chosen would never have succeeded.

Chapter 12

I will bring you back now to the year 2000. Cycling still plays a great part in our lives; gardening is another love of my life. I grow flowers and tomatoes. Ken grows the vegetables and keeps the lawn in trim. I could spend all day in the garden; the day is not long enough for all I would like to do.

We had a lovely holiday in Wales this year, around Mumbles and the Gower coast, cycling the path that borders the sea, and finishing in Swansea, walks to Bracelet Bay, sea bathing and further walks along the coastal path filled every day.

In August, Ken had a bad bout of sciatica, which put everything on hold. Pam, Roger's wife, was taken ill after returning from holiday in France, and was taken to hospital in Gloucester. The doctors did all they could for her, but to no avail. Pam died in early October that year. I did so want to see her and hold her hand. Ken was unable to drive the car at the time, and I was planning to travel to Gloucester by train, but it was too late. There was a great sadness, and I could only hold her cold hands and tell her I would look after the boys and Roger. I feel she knew I was there.

Roger has managed wonderfully in bringing up the boys since then, seeing them through university, and always being there for them. Christmas and family celebrations keep us all together as one big family; we will always be there for them and Roger for as long as they need us.

I have made several more visits to Ambridge archives to see if there is anything I have missed — letters to friends from university days perhaps? Sometimes a few chosen words can reveal more than a multitude of chitchat. On my last visit, (2007) the fire alarm went off at 7am in my accommodation — the fire escape led off from our room. A member of staff rushed in to unlock the door, shouting 'Fire! Fire! Get out!' I pushed my feet into my shoes, never mind about the laces, grabbed my gilet, trousers and handbag, and I was out of the door, closely followed by others from the other rooms.

It was still quite dark outside, it was January, and the metal winding stairs were difficult. I kept a hand on the rail in case I slipped, and hoped I wasn't holding anyone up. I got to ground level with about a dozen others;

it was quite cold and there was a slight drizzle falling. We were in a sort of courtyard-cum-patio; there were wooden tables and benches. I put my trousers on over my pyjamas, the other escapees seemed to have grabbed their fleece jackets or coats — why didn't I think of that! I will next time. We waited for about ten minutes then lights began to appear in the other part of the building. One of our group said he was going back inside to see what was happening.

Just at that moment, a young man came from inside to give us the 'all clear' which was just as well as we heard afterwards there should have been a lighted sign at the bottom of the fire escape directing us to the meeting point at the front of the house, on the street outside. We would probably have been forgotten until they had a headcount. The fire brigade had not been called when the alarm went off, standard practice and company instructions had been ignored. A lot of lessons were learnt, and, for the future, corrected. As we climbed the stairs to our rooms, there was a smell of smoke — a sweet, sickly smell, someone had been smoking in the bathroom or bedroom, which was strictly forbidden.

I went to the archives that morning. They were open, but not for researching — it was obviously not my day! I retraced my steps, and although I was booked in for another night in my accommodation, I didn't really feel like being in the same room again, so I collected my things and caught the train to Kings Cross. At Kings Cross I had little time to reach Paddington and the train to Exeter. I have walked from Kings Cross to Waterloo in the past, but for this day necessity took over — I would have to tackle the Underground, where there were a few anxious moments, but I survived to tell the tale! The country mouse comes to town.

There were several more visits to Northwood. Edward took Roger and myself on a tour of the garden and down to the vegetable and fruit garden, where we sampled the raspberries. It was rather a long walk for Edward, but we rested halfway in the wood shed and sat on some logs and talked, he was too tired that evening to join us for an evening meal. I have visited Tricia, in Wales. She is writing an account of the family matriarchs and we were able to exchange notes. Robert, a cousin of Edward gave me a small book given by Andrew to Lucy in 1894. I treasure that.

A visit to Andrew's granddaughters was quite different. The younger granddaughter was very pleasant — I liked her. She gave me the address of her older sister who she said was the family archivist, but later, on the instruction of her older sister I suspect, they closed ranks. I can quite understand their position, and respect their privacy.

Northwoods was handed over to Edward's father to be passed down to himself and his brother eventually The eldest son, Edward's brother, was killed during the war and Northwoods became Edward's, which as I have said, he vowed he would never leave.

Lucy moved to Exmouth in the south of England where it was so much warmer away from the cold Northumbrian winds. Exmouth is only seven miles from West Hill, I have found the house where she spent the rest of her life, and when I walk along the beach I can imagine her doing the same.

Time moves on, it is now 2007. The grandchildren have grown up and done well. 2004, Andrew, Southampton University, BA geography, 2006, Richard, Southampton University, BSc geology, 2007, Joanna, Bristol University College of Art, BA art and animation. We attended their presentations with great pleasure. The continuation of the family line gives me quiet satisfaction, my raison d'etre.

My 'daydream' came true in 2007 playing my accordion at Sidmouth Folk Festival, sitting on the low seafront wall of the promenade, at first with trepidation, then gaining in confidence, I thoroughly enjoyed playing for my passing audience for one and half hours.

Roger has semi-retired but still assists when required in his previous position, he is interested in cycling and camping and hopes to travel in his spare time. Sue has a flock of Portland sheep she has built up, 'roaming' hens, four ageing goats she has given a good home to and an avid interest in gardening, plus part time work at Lydford National Trust. Ken has had two operations in the past eighteen months but with perseverance is doing well, we keep active, love gardening and walk often. The search for my mother's real family has led me to explore many avenues over the last ten years, university archives with records of old original letters and correspondence by past university scholars, which opened up a world of the past. There were also family diaries and specific biographies where the minute research by the authors was very informative; a second hand bookshop in Ross on Wye yielded a book of 'letters' by a paternal family member written throughout his lifetime, which was of interest to me. With all this collective information the leads led me northwards to people and places where I have visited and where I feel 'at home' and we keep in touch. I hope my mother can now feel at peace, for myself I am quietly satisfied and can let go. Letter writing has almost become a thing of the past with emails being so quick, but researchers may not be as fortunate as I.

I shall probably never know the whole truth of my distant past as, footprints were very carefully covered up, but it has been a very interesting and intriguing experience looking into the past. I know everything was done with the best intentions, we were well looked after and grew up in a lovely area — a quiet village almost cut off from the busy bustle of the outside world. The village green and the wide expanse of common, as a conservation area, it will never change.

Now in a quiet moment as in the 1920s, I can look out of my bedroom window and watch the clouds scurrying by or gently billowing in the breeze past my latticed window panes; to the left of my view are the branches of an old oak tree, a haven for many birds, not least my friendly blackbird and 'Bert' the robin; a new family of descendants of the original 'Bert' appear every year with the same traits as their forbears, ever watchful in the old oak tree for the back door to open and breakfast to appear. In the distant background are some ancient pine trees whose cones the size of teacups, which we have gathered in the past when they fall to the ground, for Christmas decorations. Three columnar golden yew trees stand 10ft tall, each one planted on the birth of a grandchild and behind them two white barked silve birch, maple, rowan and cherry trees, forming a leafy background as we inteded many years ago.

Life has been good to me — adversities? Yes, everyone has them, but in adversity you can find your strength. Don't look for blame, look for the way forward. I asked myself many years ago 'Who am I?' I think by now I have found the basic details — independent, totally trustworthy, liberally minded, bear no malice, and I will be your best mate in a crisis if you need a helping hand. In my life now I feel calm, resigned and complete.

2007, I am now 87 and my story is over for the moment, whatever lies ahead I'm ready, for now, I will relax and play myself a tune.

I would have liked to leave my story with the world in a better state for everyone, but take heart, give love and hope to your family or friends, and accept what they can give to you gratefully, if you do this, the simpler things in life will bring you comfort, I know because I've been there.

Margaret.

PER ARDUA AD ASTRA

Through adversity to the stars.

The garden at Westhayes Cottage

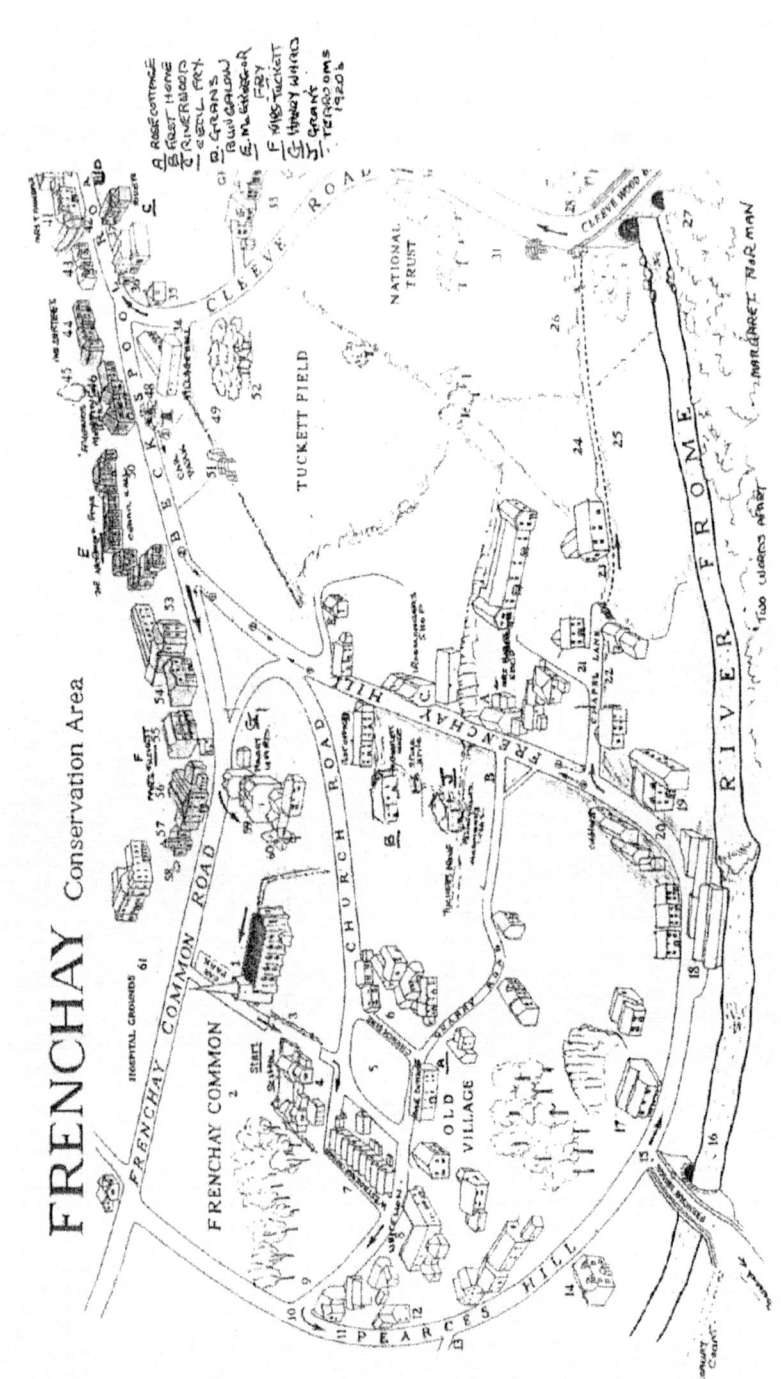

FRENCHAY Conservation Area

Key

A. ROSE COTTAGE
B. FROST HOME
C. RIVERWOOD
D. CECIL FRY
E. GRANS
F. RW GARDEN
G. E.M. GREGOR
FRY
F. MRS TUCKETT
HENRY WARD
BRANK
TERRAOOMS
1920's

CLEEVE ROAD

NATIONAL TRUST

TUCKETT FIELD

FRENCHAY HILL

CHURCH ROAD

FRENCHAY COMMON

HOSPITAL GROUNDS

OLD VILLAGE

PEARCES HILL

RIVER FROME

90

1938 – Easter in Branscombe, Devon

1938 – My first tent (Blacks) x

1985 – Rigg Beck, Lake District

1986 – Montresor, France

1988 – Campsite at Argentat, Gorge de la Dordogne

Westhayes Cottage

BRITTANY

"TWO WORLDS APART" MARGARET WERMAN

BR
Cycle Camping

Route
Towns en route
Campsites (●)

● Campsites